How to make Latex Clothes

Published by Goldust

A CIP catalogue record for this book is available from the British Library.

ISBN 978-0-9934481-0-2

Prepared and printed by:

York Publishing Services Ltd
64 Hallfield Road
Layerthorpe
York YO31 7ZQ

Tel: 01904 431213

Website: www.yps-publishing.co.uk

ABOUT THE BOOK

This book's simple objective is to show you how to make latex clothes at home, with the minimum of fuss and expense, just the most enjoyment. You do not need to have any experience or knowledge.

This book is designed with an easy to use, step by step guide, helping you to make your own bespoke latex clothes. Latex clothing is not only on the vanguard of fashion, easy to make but it is fun.

Since starting, I've won many prizes, been on catwalks, in shows and been asked to be a general manager of a leading manufacturer, where I stayed for a couple of years. In 2007, I officially started the United Kingdom's first Latex Workshops – www.LatexWorkShops.com. These have had an international attendance and many recommendations.

All words that are in *italics* can be found in the helpful glossary at the end.

With special thanks to

Mark	Photographer – MDGphotography.co.uk
Felicity	Designer
Charlie	Actress
Simon	Designer and DJ
Damarys	Wonderful woman
Claudine	Enough said

CONTENTS

INTRODUCTION

This is an easy to follow 'how to' book demonstrating the best practices required to **Make Latex Clothes**.

Designed to expand skills, imagination and enjoyment, this book is a step by step guide which teaches everything there is to know about making latex clothes. You will obtain your goals with the minimum of fuss and expense, just the most enjoyment. All in the comfort of your own home.

The results will not only be indistinguishable from the expensive shop-bought outfits but it will also be tailor-made to suit your style, body shape and above all, your imagination.

MATERIALS AND EQUIPMENT

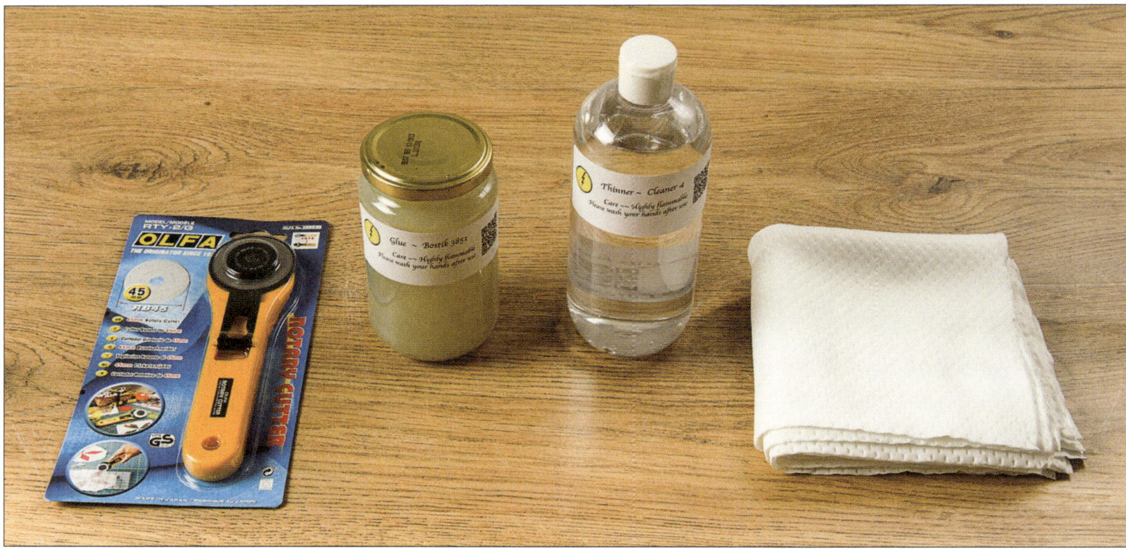

Left to right: Rotary cutter – 45mm, Glue – Bostik 3851, Cleaner 4 – Bostik 6009 (known as *Thinner*), Lint-free cloths

Left to right: Gel pen – white is the best colour, Spatulas – never use a brush, Roller – plastic or wooden (these are used for rolling wallpaper into corners), Tweezers

Left to right: Scissors, Safety pin, Superglue , Talcum powder

Left to right: Silicone spray or lubricant, Cleaning polish – Perv-O-Shine (PVC dressing aid), Wallpaper liner (for pattern cutting)

Left to right: Pencil, rubber and sharpener, Tape measure, Scotch Magic Tape, 30cm ruler

Left to right: Address labels, Latex swatch, Blu-Tack

MAKING LATEX CLOTHES

It is not difficult to make latex clothes at home, all the equipment is easy to obtain and is not so expensive.

Best results include safety first.

This is largely down to common sense and good working techniques but there are a few things to note.

When using the rotary cutter, always cut away from yourself. This outward action will not only protect you from injuries, but it will maximise your control and therefore will make cutting out the latex a lot easier. This principle should be applied to every action, even ones which might not feel right to begin with, such as marking the latex with your gel pen.

I also strongly recommend that you work in a room with good ventilation.

Your work surface

Fig 1

The starting point is a good work surface. All that you need for this is five laminated floorboards that you can easily join together. Fig 1 on the previous page. Besides being reasonably priced and available from any DIY superstore, they are very durable. The floorboards normally come in packs of ten. Easy to assemble into a large work area, plus they can be stored away into a small space. Once joined together they can be placed on any elevated sturdy surface, such as a kitchen table.

Once your work surface has been set up, you will be able to cut, clean, glue and finish your outfits with ease. However, I would recommend that you do not use silicone polish on your work surface as the silicone will prevent the glue on the seams from sticking properly.

There are professional green cutting boards, but I find them either too small or too expensive. Also, they do not fold away neatly. However, I do think they are good quality and are useful for certain, rare tasks like when you have two blades on your rotary cutter to make a parallel slit in an outfit.

STRAIGHT LINES

Step 1 Preparation

The very first thing to do is to practise cutting an oblong piece of latex into two and then gluing it back together again.

The latex should be 20cm long and 15cm wide, start with either gauge 0.4mm or 0.5mm.

Using a ruler and a white gel pen, draw a line with one continuous outward motion lengthways down the middle. See Fig 2 below.

Gel pens should be of craft quality, not from a children's store. Gel pens are used because they are clearly visible and wipe off easily without leaving any trace of a mark.

When using a gel pen do not add pressure but just glide along using the weight of the pen itself. It is very difficult to write on latex, as we would with a ball point pen.

Fig 2

Remove the ruler, hold the latex panel parallel to the line you want to cut into two, so that the rotary cutter is not cutting towards your hand. Place your thumb near the start of the line, so that it will not concertina. Place the rotary cutter on the table, allowing a 1cm space before the latex, now cut into two. This will facilitate a clean cut by preventing any concertinaing of the latex. You must always cut a line freehand, **never** using any guides, such as rulers. The latex may be stabilised by cutting parallel to your hand but, for safety, never towards yourself. See Fig 3 below. Hold the latex near to where you are going to cut it, ie next to the line and not in the middle of the panel. This will give you the most control which always means the best results. When cutting, how you hold the rotary cutter and your stance is very important. Hold the rotary cutter as though you are shaking a hand and try not to hold it like a pen, try not to place your finger on top. Stand square to the work surface, initially with your arm, straight at an angle of about 30 degrees. Use the natural weight of your shoulder to lean into cutting and do not use force from your wrist. You will soon start to bend your elbow a bit, for a more comfortable and natural feel but this is a good way to start, to get a feeling for using your shoulder. As this will give you the most control, you will have the best results from the beginning.

Fig 3

A. Mark A in the top left corner of the left panel and mark B in the top right corner of the right panel.

B. Overlap A onto B, by sliding together by approximately 1cm.

Also draw a little arrow on B, pointing towards the seam line about 2cm away from the edge of B. See Fig 4 below.

Fig 4

Turn A over and draw a little arrow 2cm away from the seam line; if turned completely over it will be on the left hand side of A. It is always very useful and a good idea to label/mark everything that you do, as you do it. Fig 5 overleaf.

Latex has an inner and an outer side. To the naked eye, the inner side appears more matt than gloss, largely because talcum powder has been applied to that side. Talcum powder is added during manufacture solely to prevent the latex from sticking to itself when being rolled ready for sale. Latex does not have any 'grain' as such but the talcum powder may run in straight lines. Fig 6 overleaf. On the left hand side is the outside, and on the right hand side is the inside, the side with a light dusting of talcum powder.

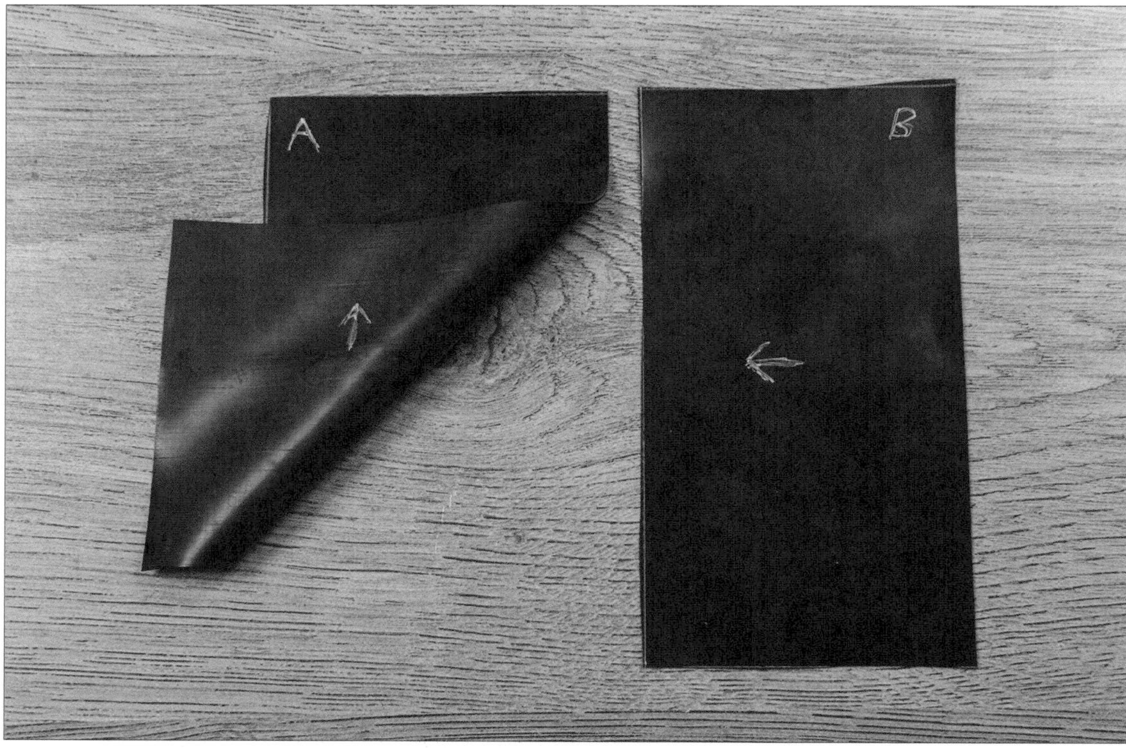

Fig 5

Fig 6

Step 2 Cleaning

Essential preparation is needed before gluing the latex back together.

Ensure that there is nothing on the latex which prevents the glue from doing its job, such as talcum powder. Therefore, the 1cm seam must be clean. Using a *lint-free cloth*, dabbed with your cleaning agent - *cleaner 4* which is known as *thinner*, in Europe - make an *anchor point* by cleaning, when the seam is horizontal to you, a 1.5cm area at the beginning of the seam line. Now move the latex so that the seam line is vertical. Then holding this *anchor point*, with one controlled action make a 1.5cm seam space, Fig 7A below and 7B overleaf.

This makes sure that there is a clean 1cm seam line. Cleaning a seam line should be done in one movement and **should not** be like stroking a pet, otherwise it will make the latex curl. Fig 7C overleaf. If this happens it means that you have to wait longer before you can apply the glue. It may also result in the surface of the latex being scratched. However, you may wipe a couple of times to remove the odd excess bit of talcum powder.

Fig 7A

Fig 7B

Fig 7C

For the best results always use a *lint-free cloth.* These are basically medical/industrial cloths that don't leave any tiny fibres behind.

Latex tends to curl if either you have wiped the latex with too much *thinner*, which is usually alcohol based, or if the latex is very thin, eg 0.25mm. In both situations, the latex will resettle on its own, usually in about 30 seconds.

Step 3 Gluing

Glue, please see the glossary for 'Glue – Latex glue,' is applied to latex with a plastic spatula. Never use a brush, as brushes can leave ridges and hairs in the seam. The best spatulas are modified store/loyalty cards, which you can customise by cutting to a width of 1.5cm. Then file the edges with a nail file, so that there are no sharp edges to damage the latex.

Store cards are 0.8mm thick, which is perfect. Credit cards are 1mm so should not be used.

A useful tip is to note or mark the spatula at a 1cm point, so that initially you can use it as a guide point when applying the *glue*.

How to hold your spatula

Hold the spatula 2cm from the gluing edge; this will give you maximum control, resulting in better accuracy. Hold the spatula as you would a pen but without your middle finger and keeping your thumb beneath your index finger. Fig 8A overleaf. Raise your index finger and squash it as flat as possible without adding too much pressure; it should be flat on the table.

The reason to have the spatula a little wider than the 1cm seam line is to allow a little bit extra *glue*, to go onto the table – a necessary step in making sure that the glue has gone to the very edge of the seam line.

It is necessary to wait at least 30 seconds before applying the *glue*, as this gives time for the *thinner* to evaporate. If you do not wait then the *thinner* will try and evaporate through the *glue* making it curl.

Dip the spatula into the *glue* just like a hen would peck. Fig 8B overleaf. Do not immerse the spatula completely into the *glue* or try to wipe off any excess, especially onto the top of the container. There should be about 4mm of *glue* vertically on the end of your spatula. Don't be concerned if there is too much or too little, just use what's there and have a go.

When applying the glue to make a seam, it is necessary to make a 1cm *anchor point* and to start from that point. This is done, as with cleaning, by firstly laying the seam horizontal to yourself. Then make a 1cm vertical *glue anchor* point at the very end.

Glue ~ Bostik 3851
Care ~~ Highly flammable
Please wash your hands after use

Fig 8A

Glue ~ Bostik 3851
Care ~~ Highly flammable
your hands after use

Fig 8B

Fig 9

The glue should go onto the work surface, Fig 9 above, so please make sure it goes both over the bottom and side of the seam. Then turn the whole seam, glued area towards you, vertical again. Be careful not to get any *glue* on the other side of your panel. You now have an *anchor point* to hold onto when making your seam line. Next place your index finger on the *anchor point*. It will prevent the panel from sliding when you are gluing and means that there will be *glue* to the very end of the seam line. Fig 10 overleaf.

Apply the *glue* as quickly as possible with a controlled firm pressure. If there is not enough *glue* to reach the end, stop and get more *glue*. Do not try and just make the *glue* last. It is much better to have a clean break point to start from again, either by turning your spatula over or dipping it into the *glue* pot again. The result should look like a snail trail on your latex.

Remember that the *glue* should actually be going a little onto the work surface, as a result of gluing to the edge of the seam. As the latex has now been effectively glued to your work surface, it must be moved immediately, otherwise the glue along the edge will set and will cause *glue-strings*, thus creating unnecessary problems later on. As you can see the left hand panel on Fig 10 overleaf has been moved a centimetre or two to prevent it from sticking to the work surface.

Fig 10

Once the *glue* has been applied **never** go over any *glued* seam line again. This would cause *glue-strings* and you would have to start again. However, if there is a point where the seam is not quite the full 1cm, especially if it didn't make it to the edge, turn the seam line so that it is horizontal to you and quickly glue that tiny area. Be careful not to lay your latex on any *glue* which has gone onto the work surface. Wipe down the work surface regularly, only using your hands. If you see any *glue-balls* on your seam line, they must be immediately removed with tweezers. I have dedicated an entire section to problems to avoid which can be found on page 30.

If after applying *glue* to the seams, they appear to curl a little or are wavy or unsightly, refrain from unfurling them or even trying to flatten them while the glue is still wet. Fig 11 opposite. Always wait until the *glue* dries before attempting to carefully separate the stuck latex, preferably with a pair of tweezers. Avoid using your fingers because the result will not look good.

Cleaning and gluing is called *prepping* your seams, you should always *prep* both pieces of latex that you are going to join.

Fig 11

The seam line in Fig 11 above has curled due to either too much *glue* or applying the *glue* too soon after applying the *thinner*.

Step 4 Ready to join

When is a seam line ready? The answer is when it is dry.

How long it takes to dry depends on a number of variable factors, from the humidity of the room to the thickness of the latex. Usually, five minutes should be enough. Although seam lines may be left overnight and will still stick perfectly the next day.

To test when seams are dry – tap them

The best way is to tap lightly, not to take finger prints. If the glue sticks to your finger-tips, then it is an indicator that the glue is still wet, if it doesn't, then it means that the glue is dry.

A useful observation is that wet seam lines look very shiny. Sticking wet glue together would be difficult and is very unforgiving of any mistakes. It would not be possible to cleanly peel apart the seam for a second chance, as it would end up with lumpy *glue-strings* and you would have to start again.

Dry seam lines have a pale shine, like a snail's trail. Waiting until the seam is dry will allow the seam to be peeled apart without the glue becoming lumpy, so there is the opportunity to correct any errors. An example of *glue-strings* is on page 30.

Step 5 Making a seam

Start by having the right latex panel as the bottom panel; so the seam will be on the left hand side.

You need to start with an *anchor point*. Carefully align the first 1.5cm of the seam edges together making sure that they are starting out in the same direction, Fig 12A below. Then overlap 1cm, join with your right thumb which will be the start of your seam. Fig 12B opposite. This now means that you will join them together knowing that they are both starting out in the same direction.

Fig 12A

Fig 12B

After this starting point, create a seam line using the *caterpillar technique*. Make sure your right thumb has joined the latex making an *anchor point*, then rest your right palm and fingers over the right bottom panel to stabilise it.

Your left hand should hold the left panel in the air so that the seams do not join together yet. Fig 12B above.

Soon you will be using your right hand index finger to gently join the seam line. Use your left hand to guide the top panel, left or right, to make a 1cm seam line. Ensure that when holding the latex you do not pull or stretch the latex. This is very commonly done to help get a straight line but stretching will make the outfit look very unsightly.

An example of stretching and other commonly encountered problems will be dealt with later in the book; Step 8, on page 30.

Panel A

The top latex panel, which you marked A will be on the left side. It should be held on the seam line, 4-5cm along and up 1cm above the seam line. Make sure that you grip the left panel seam in between your thumb and the first digit of your index finger, holding the latex 1cm above the seam. Rest your left hand middle finger on the seam to give a good direction. You can always move left and right to ensure you have a 1cm seam line, if required. It is a very straightforward method.

When joining, never raise the top panel to look at the seam line – it will actually make it quite difficult to join the panels and you will end up stretching the top panel and seam.

Your right hand index finger should now, starting from your *anchor point*, gently stroke the seam lines together, gliding along, not pressing down too hard. Your index finger should be flat and at a 90 degree angle going away from yourself.

Fig 13A below is starting at the *anchor point* and 13B opposite is creating a seam. Try and make your index finger go at a 90 degree angle. When your index finger has reached your left thumb, stop.

Fig 13A

Fig 13B

Fig 13C

Once your index finger has reached your left thumb, Fig 13C on the previous page, stop and bring the thumb of your right hand up to create a new *anchor point* and then move your right hand supportively along. Only then move your left hand, as before, another 4-5cm along and up 1cm above the seam line. Repeat your actions. Your right hand index finger should now be moving like a *caterpillar*. Fig 13D below and Fig 13E opposite. You will soon become adept at making seams – the trick is not to press too hard with your index finger.

Fig 13D

Everything should go in a straight line away from you, so if you are joining a curve, move the seam or stand differently. Double check that there is a 1cm seam line by occasionally rolling your index finger at a 90 degree angle either way on your seam line. If you can feel the edge of the latex panels, on either side of your fingernail, then that is about 1cm – a good seam line.

Do not worry about sealing the seams together, this will be done next with a roller. You should initially focus on attaching the panels with a good seam line.

Once the seams have been joined together, whether straight or curved, the ends should, of course, be the same length. Do not be concerned if it is a little out – that's very common. There is normally a couple of millimetres difference over 20cm. When making an outfit it is more enjoyable getting things right first time but it is always fun to try out new ideas

Fig 13E

with latex because it is very forgiving. As with life, when making your outfit the important thing is to try. As the seams have only just been joined, this is the best time to make any corrections. It is easy to separate and rejoin the seams again without any ill effect if you used dry seams.

When you are satisfied, then it is time to seal the seams. Start by gently rolling the seam lines and escalate your action to vigorous rolling along the seam line. Fig 14 overleaf. Always begin on the outside, as this is what people see first. Always start either top/down or from the centre/out. Every action should be from the top/down as when your seams have been joined if there is any discrepancy at the bottom it can be dealt with but if there is any difference at the top it will cause difficulties. Remember, it is always better to avoid problems rather than try to fix them.

The purpose of rolling is to force out any *air bubbles* and push the glue to the very edge of the seam, making an everlasting join.

Fig 14

To achieve a professional finish, immediately clean off any excess glue by simply sprinkling some talcum powder along the seam line. Fig 15A opposite. Rub it in with your fingers. Fig 15B opposite. This will stick to the glue. That is why we had to clean the talcum powder off in the first place.

Then, firmly wipe off the talcum powder with a *lint-free cloth* that has been dabbed with *thinner*. Fig 15C overleaf. As always, this should be a single stroking action away from yourself.

Failure to properly remove the excess glue would result in unsightly snail like streaks. If there are any large bits of glue which require more than one wipe, remove them by wiping from the top panel to the bottom panel so that you are not wiping *thinner* along and possibly into the seam line; as that would weaken the seam. Always try to wipe as little as possible and be careful not to scratch the top of the latex by rubbing too much or too hard.

At this point, you should check to see if you have a hair line of talcum powder along your seam line. If so, it means the glue is up to the edge of your seam line. Well done! You have achieved the perfect finish. Fig 15D overleaf.

Fig 15A

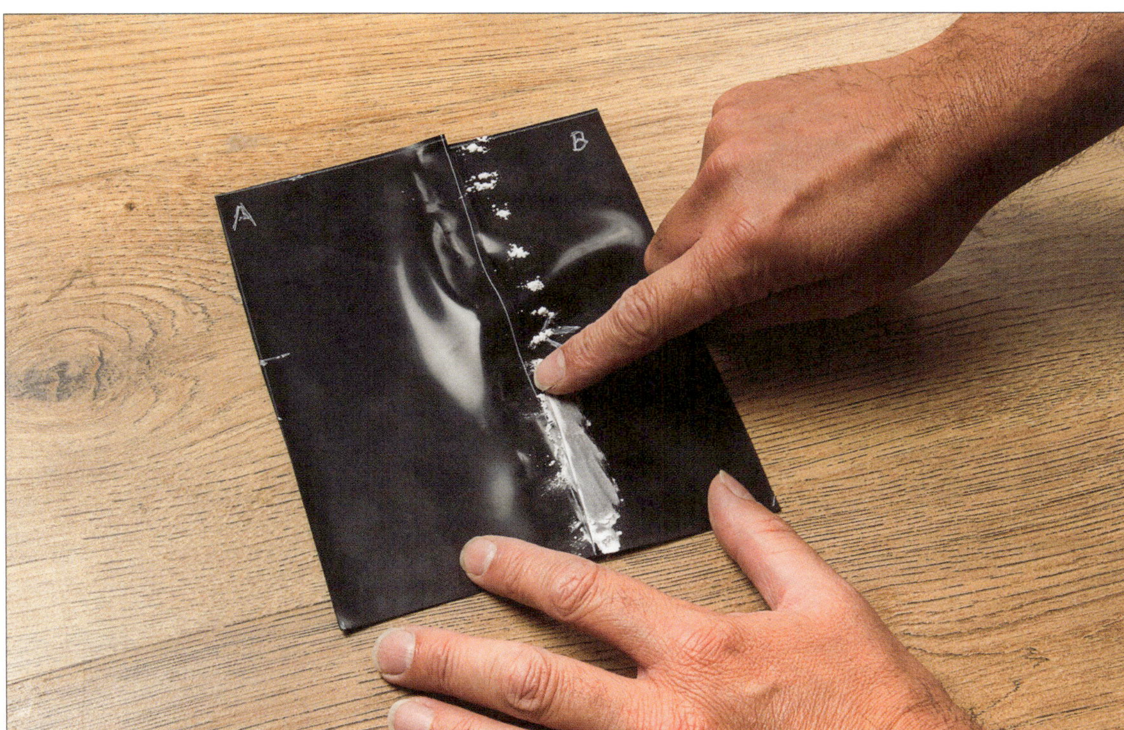

Fig 15B

Fig 15C

Fig 15D

Any and all talcum powder and gel pen lines are easily removed with *Perv-O-Shine*. We will be doing this later.

Step 6 Testing

Once the seams have been joined, you can test if you've done a good job. Position the seam line vertically, hold the latex in the middle (**not** at the corners), and pull as hard as you can. If you have joined the seams properly you will not be able to pull the panels apart. Fig 16 below.

Testing at this stage is just for fun and to build your confidence. You won't need to apply this technique to every outfit.

Amazingly, the seam can still be easily separated from either seam end. And you will be able to rejoin the seam again and it will still last for ever.

The ends of seams give way to stress very easily. So you need to add a *stress point guard*.

Fig 16

Step 7 Stress points and stress point guards

Stress points are simply where there is likely to be a lot of pressure, tension or stretching upon a concentrated area. There are various common stress points in an outfit: at the ends of seams, under the *armscye* (armhole) and at the crutch. Please check for other stressed areas like around the V of a halter-neck dress, or shirt. To protect your outfit from splitting it is necessary to add *stress point guards* to reinforce vulnerable areas. *Stress point guards* are always added on the inside.

Simply *prep* the end of the seam as usual and also a separate small semi-circle of latex to be used as a *stress point guard*. Using the *caterpillar technique*, join the semi-circle to the main seam in order to stop the seams separating, ensuring that the semi-circle is in the middle of the stress point and not in the middle of the seam. Allow a little to go over the end, to cut off later. This gives a perfect edge. A curved edge *stress point guard* should always be used, so that there are no corners or edges that can catch on anything and cause the *stress point guard* to come off. Also, semi-circles look nicer and they demonstrate a professional attention to detail. Fig 17 below.

Fig 17

I have used a yellow *stress point guard* in this photograph, solely to make it easier to see. Normally, it would be the same colour as the latex. Make sure it is added the appropriate way around. A common mistake is to apply a *stress point guard* with the outside (glossy) showing on the inside (matt). It's a small mistake but one that can easily be avoided.

Before trying on any outfit that may have a stress area, check that you are not at risk of damaging your outfit. For instance if you are making a top with a V-neck, always ensure that it has a *stress point guard*. My V *stress point guard* is not semi-circular but rather is soft V shaped so that any subtle indentation that shows through will be in the same style and flow of the outfit. Naturally, any visible *stress point guard* excess will be cut off. Fig 18 below.

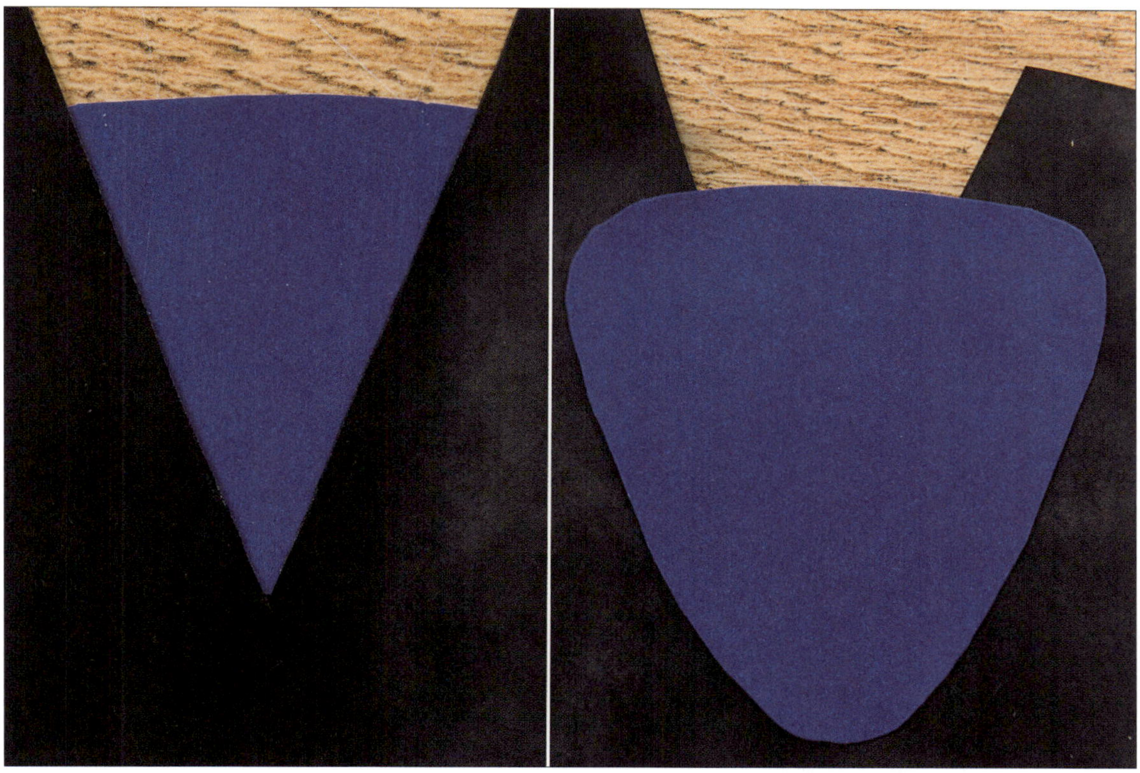

Outside Inside *Fig 18*

As well as classic *stress point guards* you can also be creative and use trim instead.

Step 8 Problems to avoid

Be careful not to get **any dirt**, such as tiny *glue-balls*, onto seams. If this happens then they will have to be removed with a pair of tweezers. If latex has been joined together with a wet seam and then pulled apart it will have *glue-strings* or *glue-balls* and so you would have to start at Step 2 again. Fig 19 below.

Fig 19

In the case of *air bubbles* try to remove them by gently rolling them to an edge. If this method doesn't work, pierce the *air bubble* in the middle of one side with a safety pin and gradually allow/squeeze the air out. Fig 20 opposite.

Fig 20

Rolling too vigorously or when joining your seam at a sharp angle.

Fig 21A

A *mountain kink* is a prominent fold on one side of a seam line. It might occur when making a 3D seam, when gluing the *armscye*. As will be explained soon, if your thumbs are touching during this process, it should prevent kinks. When rolling the seams, after joining them together, if you initially roller too vigorously to seal them, you might cause a kink. Fig 21A on the previous page and Fig 21B below.

The result if you do not keep your thumb together when gluing your sleeve. *Fig 21B*

If it's simply not possible to undo the seam and re-glue then you can try to at least make it look better. To do this hold either side of the *mountain* kink and stretch the top and bottom seam as far apart as possible. Then squeeze the kink together. This will result in a *hill kink* rather than a *mountain kink*; more of a general lump, it will not really be so noticeable on 3D seams.

To be perfect, just practise and concentrate on what you are doing. Prevention is much better than any cure.

Fig 22 on the opposite page is the result of the top panel being stretched into a straight line. If you stretch latex to get a straight line for joining, it will look terrible. You just have to guide the top panel by easing it left or right to maintain a 1cm seam line. It is, of course, the same for the bottom seam line. Do not pull into a straight line otherwise it will have the same effect.

Fig 22

Fig 23

Fig 23 on the previous page shows when you have added too much glue to make a seam line. It means that you will have to waste time and risk damaging your outfit cleaning it off. Everyone has a learning curve but it is better to learn from others' mistakes than waste your own time.

You can now make latex clothes

CURVED LINES

Step 9 Curves and large seam lines

Using the same size of latex as for the straight line seam in Step 1. Draw an S line, label, cut and *prep* in exactly the same way as you did for the straight line. Fig 24A below.

Place your thumb near the start of the line so that it will not concertina. Place the rotary cutter on the work surface, allowing a 1cm space before the latex. Now cut the panel into two. You will have to move the latex a little and/or move your body position a little to get a clean cut. As usual cut away from yourself and try to be at a 90 degree angle. Remember that you must always cut a line freehand and **never** use any guides, such as rulers or flexi-curves.

The latex may be stabilised by cutting parallel to your hand, please never towards yourself. Fig 24B overleaf.

Fig 24A

Fig 24B

Next, label the panels A and B, as before. The right panel, B, will be the bottom panel and so the seam will be on the left hand side. Label everything as you go along.

When creating your seam, practise the *caterpillar technique* but really concentrate on getting a 1cm seam line. This will mean that you will have to pull the top panel, left and right at the seam. Do not worry if the seam does not lie flat. This is solely due to the shape of the seam line. Concentrate on getting support for the underneath panel, in particular the immediate next 4-5cm that you are going to join. You will have to do this by making sure your left hand middle finger is on the panel B seam. If you try to use your right hand to reach out and hold the bottom panel down this may impinge on your *caterpillar* index finger movement. So you must use your left hand middle finger to hold the seam line area about 6cm in front. Naturally when you are joining with your left hand everything is mirrored. Do not stretch the top or bottom seam line, just guide/pull the top panel left or right. It may be that your seam goes out by 0.2cm and it is not always possible to get back to a 1cm seam line within 1cm but you will be able over the next 2-3cm. Everything becomes easier with experience.

Having the most control means achieving the most professional finish. When joining your *anchor point* on your seam, it is easier when the top seam has the least movement. If you try and hold a protruding triangle shape then it will move/wiggle a lot. In order to achieve this, it may mean that you have to turn both panels over. Having this extra control will reflect in the quality of your finished outfit. Just do not forget that you must join seams from top/down.

When working with a big panel, a large seam line or a particularly curved one, it can be rather troublesome, if not impossible, to hold or position all of the top panel to stop the top seam from joining onto the bottom seam or even onto itself. Just insert some standard letter paper in between the seams as a barrier. This is a useful tip which can prevent problems developing. Fig 25 below.

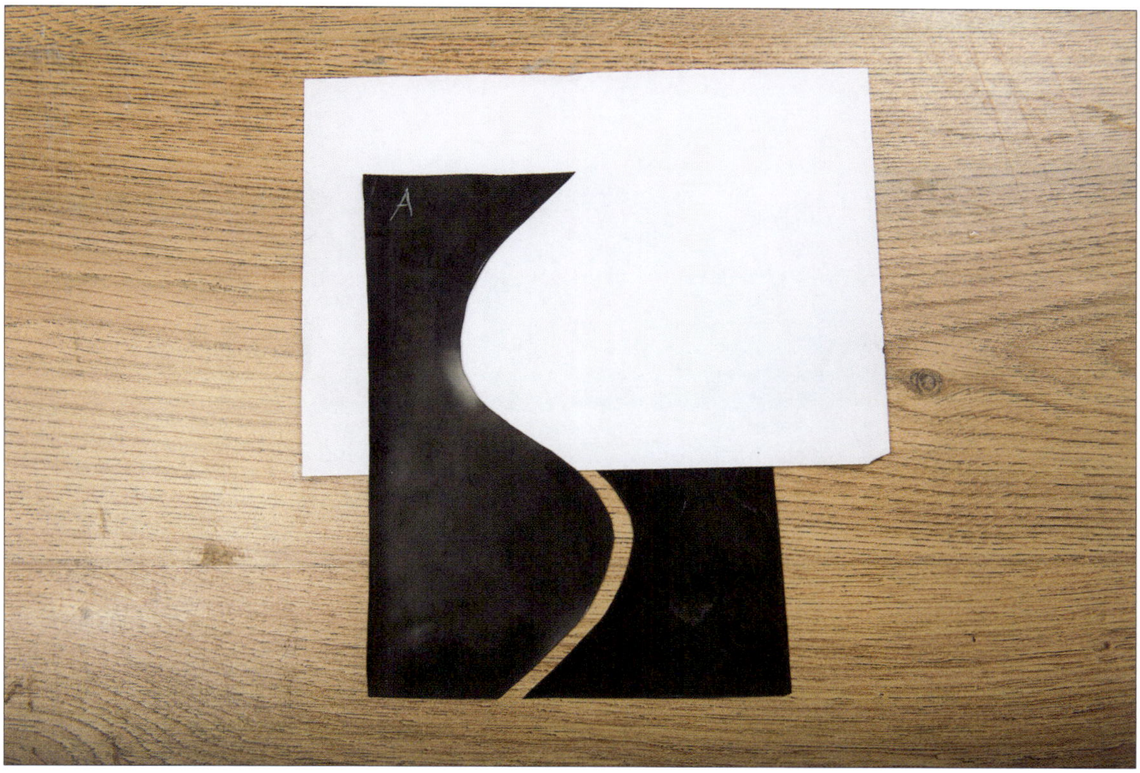

Fig 25

CREATING 3D SEAMS ON A 2D SURFACE

Using the same size of latex as for the straight line seam in Step 1, draw the general shape of the head of a sleeve and a shoulder seam line. Label and *prep* using the same method as for the straight line. Fig 26 below.

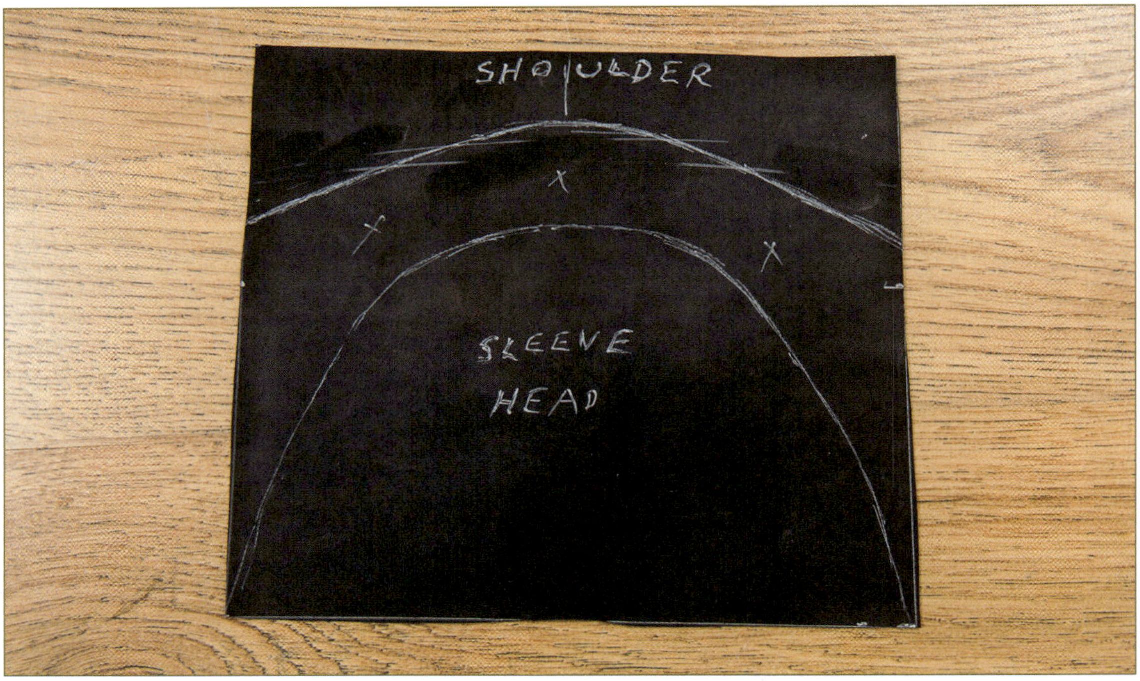

Fig 26

Joining the sleeve head seam requires a different approach than before due to the extreme curve. The *caterpillar technique* isn't suitable, instead you should use the *rolling technique*.

Remember the best working practice that latex should always be joined top/down, front/back, centre/out.

Step 10 Preparing and joining 3D seams

If a seam starts at one end and finishes at the other, it is likely that one panel will be slightly longer than the other. The difference will all be on one side of your panel either the front or the back. This will not give the best fit, for example, having extra latex at the chest line. The way to reduce the difference, if not eliminate it completely, is by gluing centre/out. Fig 27 opposite. You will soon become completely ambidextrous.

Fig 27

Following the top/down rule, the shoulder panel will be over the sleeve panel. However, for joining them together place the shoulder panel underneath, starting on the left hand side with the seam on the right. The sleeve head panel on the upper right hand side. Fig 27 above. Use a sheet of paper to separate the bottom half of the seam. Make an *anchor point* in the middle of the *armscye*, using your left hand thumb, the same as previous procedures.

Step 11 The secret to perfect seams

The secret of making perfect seams **is simply to make sure that, at all times, the bottom panel seam line is in a straight line but not stretched.** For an *armscye* it means that the left hand is having to manipulate the next 2-3cm of the panel into a straight line without stretching it, you have to use your left hand index finger to do this. It doesn't matter what temporarily happens to the rest of the outfit. The left thumb is the *anchor point* as normal. Fig 28A overleaf.

Make sure that your right thumb touches your *anchor point.* Then with your right thumb ensure that the edge of the upper panel touches your thumb nail on the inside bottom corner. Fig 28B overleaf.

Fig 28A

Fig 28B

Fig 28C

Now gently press down so that you can feel that the outer edge of the underneath panel is under your thumb nail, on the outside bottom corner. Fig 28C above.

Next roll your thumb at an angle of 45 degrees, away from yourself and onto the bottom panel, into a 1cm seam. Fig 28D overleaf. It is easier if you clench your fist when rolling.

Once done, you should immediately move your *anchor point* along. Your thumbs should be touching most of the time and you should roll the top latex into making a 1cm seam, never stretching or pulling the latex. Also, be very careful not to *jump*, if you start too far away from the *anchor point* in between rolls, as this will result in *kinks*. Be mindful about *kinks*: if there is one, sort out the problem immediately. Always make sure that the bottom latex has about a 2-3cm straight line waiting for the top latex panel. This procedure is called the *rolling technique*.

I cannot overstate the importance of not stretching the latex. Carry on until finished. The latex seam line will undulate quite a lot, but this is a good sign as you are working on a 3D shape on a 2D surface. Next turn the sleeve head around and do the other half. Your hands will obviously have to switch roles.

Fig 28D

Fig 29A

The right thumb is the *anchor point* and the index finger makes a straight line with the seam. Fig 29A opposite. Make sure that the edge of the upper panel touches the inside bottom corner of your thumb nail. Fig 29B below. If it doesn't then, you will find your seams start to get very thin.

Gently press down so that you can feel that the outer edge of the underneath panel is under the outside bottom corner of your thumb nail. Fig 29C overleaf.

Now roll your thumb at an angle of 45 degrees, going away from yourself and onto the bottom panel, into a 1cm seam. Fig 29D overleaf.

As usual, roll, apply talcum powder and clean off any excess glue as illustrated in Step 5. Be careful when rolling the seam, as it is not flat. You should hold the seam so that the couple of centimetres you are rolling are going over a smooth arc. Fig 30 overleaf.

Once finished, the armscye will look either ruffled or lifted off of the work surface. Both are what you should expect as it is a 3D seam. When you wear your outfit, it will fit perfectly. Fig 31 overleaf.

Fig 29B

Fig 29C

Fig 29D

Fig 30

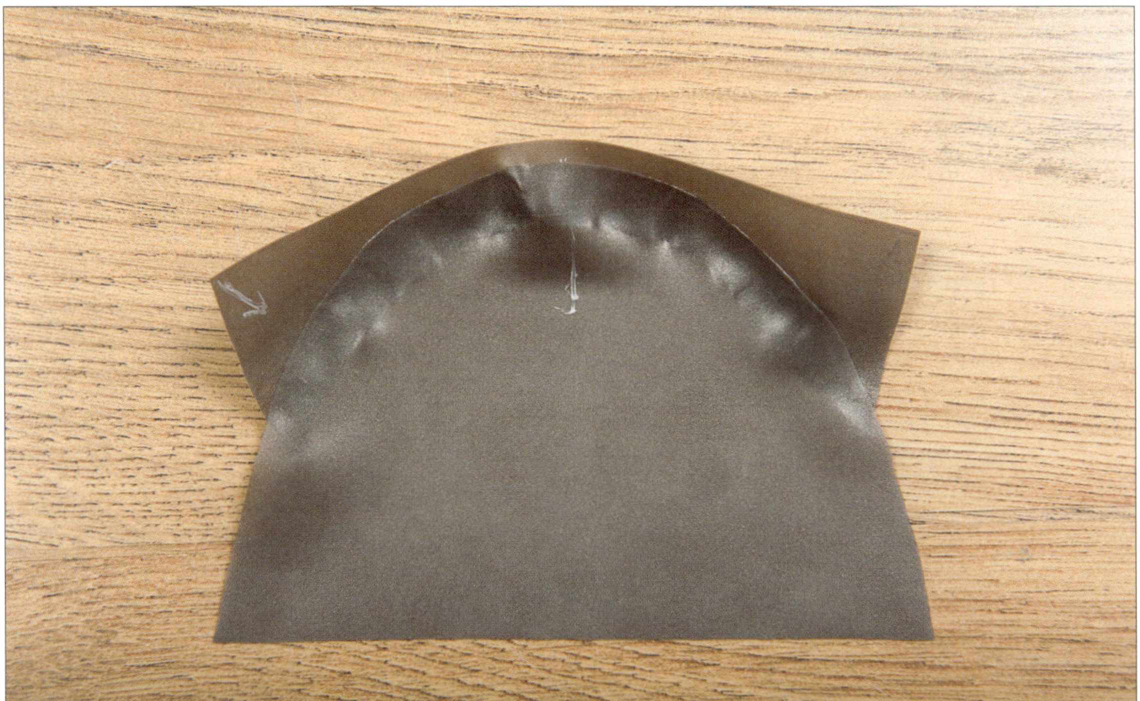

Fig 31

HOW TO ENHANCE CLOTHES

Appliqués

Appliqués are extra designs, normally of latex, that can be stuck onto the surface of the outfit, although any material can be used. All that really needs to be remembered is that appliqués might restrict movement. Appliqués can be used to advantage, for example to emphasise a cleavage or to tighten a waist area.

Before attaching appliqués it is advisable to first finish your outfit. This will enable you to predict how the appliqués will look on the finished outfit and ensure you achieve the correct fit.

When cutting appliqués from latex, always use a rotary cutter to obtain a clean edge. Scissors and scalpels can easily leave a jagged edge which would be prone to splitting or tearing. The simplest way to get the best appliqué is to print your appliqué onto an address label, then stick that onto your latex and cut it out. You can use art labels but there is no need for the extra expense. Fig 32A below shows a printed label and Fig 32B opposite shows your appliqué ready to be cut.

Fig 32A

Fig 32B

Fig 33

The label gives a clear line to cut and restricts the elasticity, therefore giving a much more accurate appliqué; it's easier to cut accurately. Fig 33 on the previous page.

When adding appliqués to the outfit start either centre/out or top/down, depending on the appliqué. For large appliqués the *paper separation* technique is recommended. When doing so, use a single piece of paper. When I made some full body wings and I needed to glue everything, I used some 1m width wallpaper liner, which is also very good for pattern cutting; it's cheap and available from DIY centres.

Very large appliqués can be just glued on the outside edges. This will give a smooth, perfect looking finish. Otherwise you may see the glue lines across the appliqué.

Appliqués are not only for the outside of an outfit. You can make a shaped hole and glue your appliqué on the inside. Fig 34 below. I once had a hole in an outfit and rather than just fixing the problem like you would if using a bicycle repair kit, I customised the hole and added a shaped appliqué onto the inside. This gave a much more interesting look. The appliqué was the same shape as the hole, as you always notice some indentation.

Fig 34

In case the appliqué that you want is too difficult to draw or even cut then you may want to search online and with permission copy a pattern or perhaps create your own design. Save your image in an appropriate file format and then have it laser-cut. Most universities provide this laser-cutting service at an affordable cost. Alternatively browse the Internet to find laser printers in the area where you live.

Laser printers usually cut 1m square panels and so you can design everything within that perimeter.

You can also have non-latex appliqués as will be expanded on, in Step 26. Adding non-latex materials.

Keyholes

You can also decorate your outfits by inserting holes in different patterns. You can create amazing designs for example, around the cleavage, or along the length of your outfit.

When making any sort of hole, you should apply a *stress point guard* to reinforce it. It is much easier and quicker to add the *stress point guard* before cutting the 'hole'. Fig 35 below.

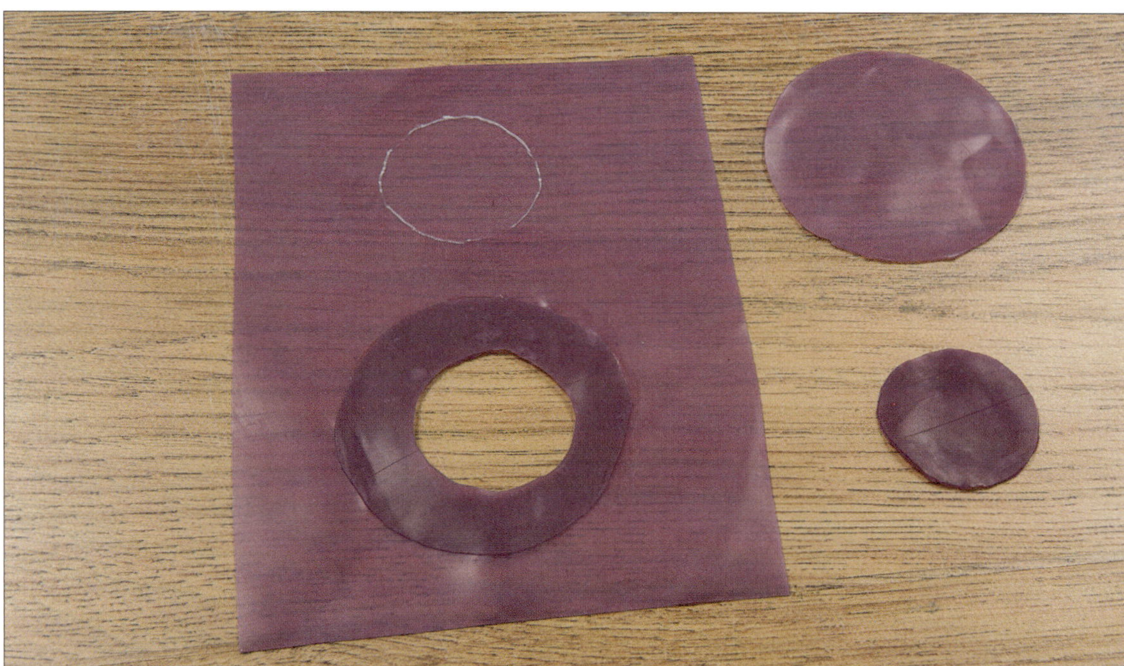

Fig 35

This shows the original large *stress point guard* and the hole with the 'scrap' cut out. There are more ideas for appliqués and keyholes further on under the heading Repairs.

Pleats and ruffles

Introduction

The most common types of pleats are the knife pleat and the box pleat. In Fig 36 below you can see four box pleats in the middle with directional knife pleats on either side. These are very simple to make and can add a lot of individual style to an outfit.

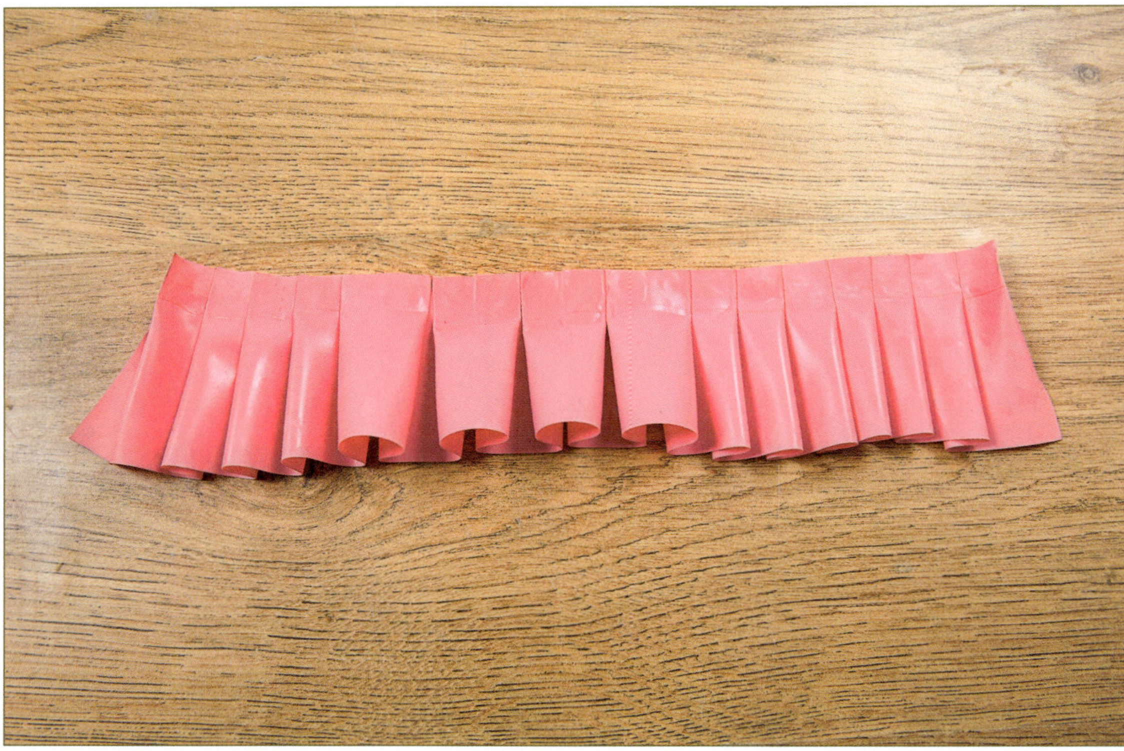

Fig 36

The seam needs to be *prepped* on both sides. Make sure that the seam has been labelled correctly by drawing seam arrows with your gel pen on each side of the latex panel.

Once the usual 1.5cm of both top sides have been cleaned, apply the glue to the first side. Best practice is to wait until that glue dries before turning that side over and laying it on the work surface. If you wish, you can apply some *cling film* to just the glued seam. This will stop it sticking to anything and not affect the glue on the glued seam. Then turn it over immediately and carry on. Personally, I find *cling film* can be troublesome as it often sticks to itself. I also find the flow rate of applying the glue over latex and the little bit of *cling film* to be noticeably different. This interferes with the application of the glue, by not allowing the spatula to flow freely over the seam surface. As a result glue tends to drag onto the *cling film* and consequently veers off the seam line. For these reasons I choose to avoid the *cling film* method and prefer to wait. Fig 37 below shows *cling film* on a seam line.

Fig 37

The first time I made a pleat, I carefully marked out every point where I needed to fold my seam. However, I very soon discovered that when folding the seam it was very difficult to to be exact. This meant the next *fin* was even more a little off of the mark. Soon the marks were redundant.

Now I measure the width of pleats using a different constant measure, the width of my thumb. For smaller pleats I can always make a mark on my thumb and work to that scale.

Step 12 Knife pleats - upwards

This is a professional, quick way which gives perfect results

When making pleats the formula is to use 3:1, for example, a 100cm strip of latex yields about 33cm of pleats.

Holding your strip of latex at one end and the seam 90 degrees away from you, so it is vertical, allow the latex hang freely with the help of gravity. Place your right thumb at a right angle to the inside top end of the seam, then fold it over and stick the width of the right thumb outwards. See Fig 38A below, Fig 38B and Fig 38C opposite.

Still using your right thumb, hold the seam line immediately below the pleat line at 90 degrees, then place your left thumb directly underneath your right thumb. This is space 1. Fig 38D overleaf.

Move your left thumb down along the seam, starting and including space 1, three spaces to space 3. Including space 1 it will be a total of three thumb nail widths. Fig 38E overleaf.

Fig 38A

Fig 38B

Fig 38C

Fig 38D

Fig 38E

Next touch your thumb nails together, by folding the gap inwards, so that the *fin* created protrudes with equal measure. Fig 38F below. You can use fingers from either hand to push the seam inwards to get this result. The aim is to touch your thumb nail edges together.

Fig 38F

Remove your upper, original, right thumb and join that *fin* you have just created into that empty space. Fig 38G overleaf. Repeat this process for more upward knife pleats.

To make a row of pleats there are very few instructions – they just have to be repeated. Place your right thumb at right angles just below the last pleat and your left thumb immediately below your right thumb. Count three thumb spaces, starting and including space 1 and stopping on the third thumb space. Create an equal sided inward *fin*, remove your right thumb and fold the *fin* upwards into the empty gap.

These skills are an asset which will be helpful when making your bespoke outfits.

Fig 38G

Step 13 Knife pleats – downwards

Creating knife pleats, folding downwards, is the same process as in Step 12 **except** there is no need to have your right thumb covering an empty space under the pleat, as you did when folding upwards, as you do not need to leave a space. Have your right thumb **on** the pleat. As before, measure three thumb spaces, resting your left thumb on the third thumb space. Fold the *fin* inward, as before and simply stick downwards.

Step 14 Box pleats

Box pleats are simply two knife pleats, in opposite directions: one going up and one going down. It is that straight forward. All *fins* will be inwards. Start off by making an upward pleat exactly as in Step 12. Then make a downwards pleat as in Step 13 and you have a box pleat, as shown in Fig 39 opposite. If you would like more box pleats, just repeat the process.

Fig 39

Step 15 Rolled pleats

After learning the standard skills, there is plenty of scope for being even more creative and inventive. Fig 40 overleaf is an example of an outfit I designed. After making the collar with two layers of pleats I wanted to accessorise the front. A good way to do this was by adding some pleats. I wanted these pleats to be special and so I firstly accessorised my strip of latex with trim. Then I decided to join the pleats the full width of the strip, thereby giving them a different style. Additionally I didn't want them to be flat, I wanted them to be much more flamboyant, so I opted for *rolled pleats*. This was done by dusting a pencil with some talcum powder and sandwiching it at the top end of each *fin* during the making of the knife pleats. Once I'd completed each pleat, I easily slid the pencil out and the job was done! The glue stuck to the talcum powder, not to the other side of the latex, giving me the rolled effect – a simple variation of a knife pleat with a very distinctive look. I also overlapped them a little to give volume, for even more effect. Fig 40 overleaf.

This very simple progression has enabled me to enhance many outfits.

Fig 40

Step 16 Ruffles

Effectively these are a gentle, wavy form of a pleat. They can be used for making Elizabethan-like necklines, for adding peplums or frills on dresses or for creating flamboyant sleeves. A ruffle is simply a panel where one side of the width is significantly longer than the other.

We shall practise with a ruffle which has a 360 degree circumference at the inner seam. Take a piece of latex about 25cm square. Draw an inner 5cm diameter circle in the middle and then an outer circle which touches all of the outer edges. Do not worry if the circle does not look perfect. Next draw a straight line from the centre to the middle of any edge.

When cutting your circles, cut the inner circle first as this will give you more latex to hold, more control. If you cut off the outer circle first, then there would not be so much to hold on to for the inner circle. When cutting circles try to cut in a straight line, away from yourself, moving the latex just like an old record would go around a turntable. It doesn't have to be cut in one go. You may have to pause and gently slide the circle towards you while, very carefully, simultaneously sliding the rotary cutter trying to avoid lifting it off the table. But don't worry if you do, just be careful when you continue with your cutting.

Once you have cut both circles, you may proceed to cut the line from the centre to the edge, in order to create a strip.

Whenever cutting make sure that you are not going to damage any other part of the latex. This means you should cut from the centre to the outside, not towards any other parts of your outfit, just in case you slip and damage them. Always cut at a 90 degree angle away from yourself, for the most control.

See Fig 41A below. Figs 41B-D overleaf.

When *prepping* the inner circle: clean and glue using the same method.

Start with your *anchor point*. Then it is better to apply the *thinner*/glue only to about one third or possibly half and then stop. Next lift the entire panel and move it to a different area on the work-surface. Be very careful not to get any glue stuck on the underside. Whilst moving it, turn it 180 degrees to make completing the task much easier. Always glue in a straight line and **never** start from either end and meet in the middle. See Figs 42A-D overleaf.

Fig 41A

Fig 41B

Fig 41C

Fig 41D

Making the *anchor point.*

Fig 42A

Gluing the first half. *Fig 42B*

Carefully moving the whole panel. *Fig 42C*

After turning the panel 180 degrees, finish gluing away from yourself. *Fig 42D*

To add this panel to another you will have to use the *rolling technique*, as you learnt in Step 10 – Preparing and joining 3D seams, page 38. Firstly, the underneath panel should be *prepped*; to practise use a panel with a straight edge. The underneath panel will be on the left with the seam on the right hand side. Then add your circular panel *anchor point*. Your *anchor point* thumb should of course be your left thumb as the underneath panel is on the left. The next action is to *roll* the top panel with your right hand thumb, away from the underneath panel. Position the outer cuticle corner of your thumbnail onto the edge of the top panel seam. Then, as usual, *roll* 45 degrees away from yourself and the underneath panel. The inside bottom edge of your thumb should end up feeling the seam line edge of the bottom panel. This will make a good 1cm seam line. Simply repeat your actions and your efforts will soon result in ruffles. These instructions may seem detailed or difficult but it is a lot easier just doing it! A good tip is to try and control the ruffles of the top panel by holding the widest sides' edge, the far right edge, when *rolling*, between your end two fingers. This will help move the mass of latex out of the way of your *rolls* and so help prevent little kinks. It will soon be a natural action.

The results will be worth practising. Figs 43A-C overleaf will help.

Fig 43A

Expect ruffles not to lie flat.

Fig 43B

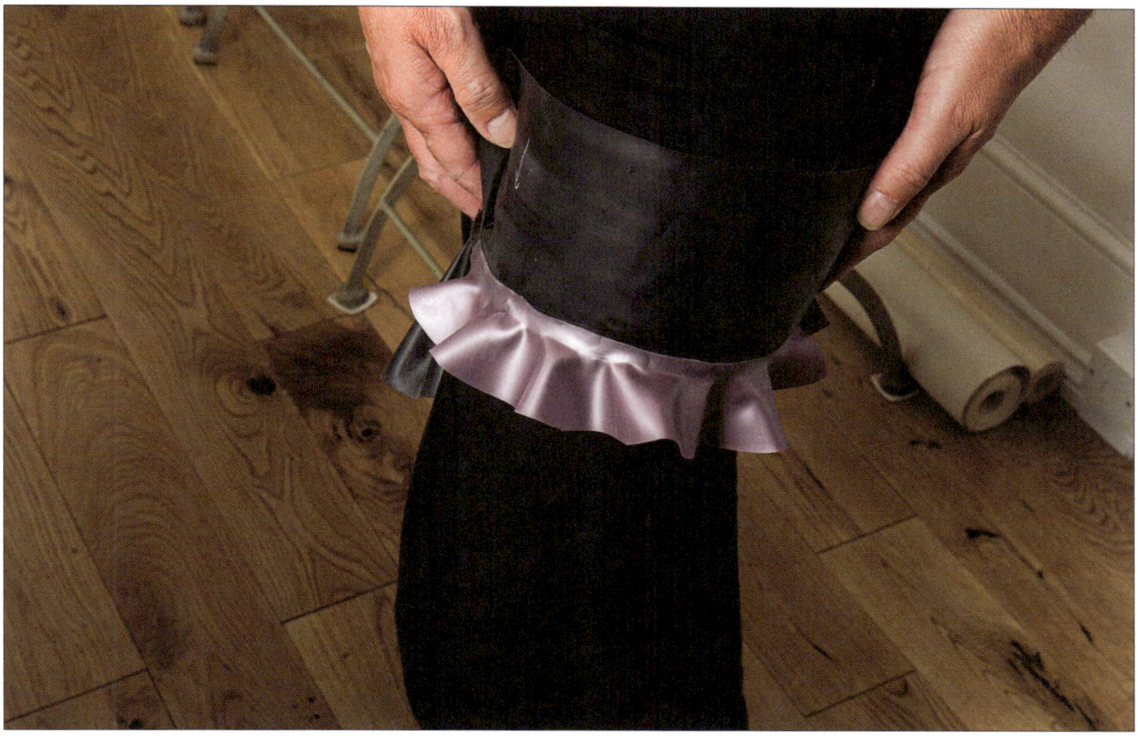

The finished look will be perfect. *Fig 43C*

If you would like to make a short skirt but would prefer it not to be too revealing, then make the end line circumference heavier: this means, apart from adding trim, the end line needs to be bigger. So instead of a ratio of 3:1 for the outer edge, you could use 5:1. Or you can think of it as making the outer edge a 450 degree circumference. You just have to cut the panels correctly, wider at the outer circle. The result would be a ruffle skirt with more weight to it meaning it would not 'fly up' as easily as one with a 360 degree edge. And the ruffles would have more depth.

HOW TO GET IN AND OUT OF YOUR OUTFITS

Usually, with a bit of wriggling and sometimes with the aid of silicone on pertinent parts of your body. You will be able to get through most reasonable openings. Even if the entrance is a round neck then you may still get in, if the latex gauge is thin enough to stretch by the *hole entry* method – this is largely a catsuit interest. This is often done by either firstly covering yourself in silicone or standing under a running shower. However, this is not the most common way to get into tight areas of an outfit. Here are some ideas for loosening part of your outfit to allow you to get into it, without it having a detrimental effect on the style or look of the outfit.

Zips

Fig 44

In Fig 44 above, from left to right: fixed length zip with diamontés, fixed length zip, stainless steel zip by the metre with the *stoppers* underneath, nylon zip by the metre and plastic zip by the metre. Next to the stainless steel *stoppers* are four stainless steel *sliders* and at the bottom is a standard soldering iron for creating plastic *stoppers*.

We use two types of zips; stainless steel or plastic. A larger toothed-plastic zip – is referred to as a plastic zip and is generally used for male outfits. A smaller toothed-plastic zip is called a nylon zip, and is generally used for women's outfits. The only difference is the size of the teeth.

A *slider* is the mechanism that moves the teeth up and down to open or close the zip.

A *stopper* is the end bit of the zip which prevents the *slider* from sliding off. *Stoppers* are already on fixed length zips. Zips bought by the metre have to have *stoppers* added to them. Stainless steel *stoppers* are available for stainless steel zips. For plastic zips, you solder the ends.

If you ever see stainless steel rivets, usually 5mm, at an end of a zip, they are only for style.

If using a zip, the first thing is to *prep* it.

Step 17 Preparing the zip

The first thing is to make sure that the zip is able to stick to the latex. The poly-cotton part will not stick to the *prepped* latex by itself so the zip must be *prepped* as well. The poly-cotton needs to be soaked in some *PVA glue* like Copydex.

Fig 45

The way this is done is by lying the zip horizontal to you. Then adding the *PVA glue* with your spatula away from yourself and at a 90 degree angle away from the teeth, in short sections. This will make sure you do not glue the teeth together. Once both sides have been glued, the PVA *glue* needs to dry. To speed this process up, place the zip onto some *tin* (aluminium) *foil* on a radiator, this will prevent the zip from staining the radiator. Once dry, now *prep* the other side of the zip. Fig 45 above.

Step 18 Adding sliders

Once the zip is dry, you may add as many *sliders* as you wish from either end. *Sliders* may also be added at opposite ends. This will allow you to make an opening mid way along the zip. When adding *sliders* make ensure that the zips teeth are clean and free from anything which might clog them. Then add one half of the zip to the *slider* until the teeth have reached the widest part of the *slider*. Then add the other half of the zip to the other half of the *slider*, in the same way. This is the point that the teeth start to engage. Fig 46A below.

Adding the first half of the zip up to the widest part of the *slider*. *Fig 46A*

Carefully press both halves of the zip, next to the slider, downwards onto the work surface. Holding the poly-cotton as close to the teeth as reasonable, pull the *slider* onto the zip. When starting it is much easier if you wiggle or just oscillate the *slider* a bit. This may seem difficult at first, but you will soon acquire the skill to add the *slider* with natural ease. Fig 46B overleaf.

Fig 46B

The *slider* is now on but you will notice the *slider* is upside down and so simply turn the whole zip 180 degrees around. Apply as many sliders as you wish.

Fig 46C

Fig 46C above illustrates the successful addition of a *slider* to the zip.

Step 19 Adding stoppers

Stoppers for stainless steel zips are readily available from any haberdashery and they are used to ensure that the *sliders* remain firmly within the zip and that they do not slide off. Both ends of the zip must be secured.

For fixed length stainless steel zips, you can remove these *stoppers*, add *sliders* and then add some new *stoppers* again.

Stoppers applied to stainless steel zips can be tightened with a pair of pliers.

Plastic zips need to be secured by following these easy steps :

You should solder the bottom zip sides together and the top sides individually.

1. Starting from the outer side, which people will see, solder the bottom three teeth, on each side, all together.

2. Using a stroking motion, centre/out, stroke these teeth until you can feel them sink in a little. This normally happens after three to tour strokes before you achieve a perfect finish.

3. Then turn the zip over and repeat the procedure. Careful not to pause or push down too hard. At the top end, solder the individual sides, three teeth together once again.

It is important not to apply too much pressure when using the stroking motion. The plastic must be stroked in the same manner as you would draw a line in pencil. Fig 47 overleaf shows how the plastic/nylon zip should look after being soldered.

For zips by the metre at the top of the zip it is a good idea to leave a little excess which you will cut off to the exact length when you are finishing your outfit.

Just above the bottom *stopper* on both plastic and stainless steel zips, sew with some normal cotton thread, three or four times around the teeth. Fig 48 overleaf. This acts as a buffer so if the *slider* is pulled down too hard, it will not break the zip.

Fig 47

Fig 48

Step 20 Finishing off

Finally we need to tidy up the zip.

The next step is to tidy up a little. Trim the bottom of the zip so it looks neat, that is in a semi-circle. Fig 49 below shows the line to trim. If something looks neat then it demonstrates that thought has gone into an outfit. Therefore, it is likely to be more professional.

Fig 49

Leave the top of the zip for now as you will come to that when you remove any excess length. The zip is now ready.

Before adding a zip, wait until the outfit has been finished and double check the measurements to make sure that the zip is exactly in the right place, especially if the zip is being inserted into a panel rather than being joined to a side seam line. If it is being joined to the edge of a side seam, like the centre zip in a catsuit pattern, then it is straight forward centre/out procedure. The *stress point guards* will be long strips supporting either side of the zip and not to forget you need to add one at the bottom of the zip.

If the zip is being joined to the middle of a panel then you must take care. Zips normally go in the middle and if only a few millimetres out may look a little odd. So wait until you have finished your outfit then double check that the zip is in the right place before cutting.

The outfit must have a 5mm oblong gap where the teeth are going to go. So from any centre line measure out 2.5mm either side and cut that groove. The bottom *stopper* should be included within the oblong space otherwise it will uncomfortably press into your back and look like a lumpy *glue-ball*.

We now need to *prep* 2.5cm all the way around the inside of the zip gap. Join the zip to your panel from the centre/out, i.e., from the bottom of the zip to the top end line using the *caterpillar technique* as usual.

Next add a *stress point guard*. It usually will go all of the way around the zip, as the zip is usually not too long. You need a 1cm lengthways gap in the centre, for the teeth to open, so will be in a U shape. The *stress point guard* on one side should be joined 1cm onto the main panel and about 0.75cm on the zip, so a total width of 4.5cm. The length is simply the length of the zip, plus 2.5cm for the bottom *stress point guard*. You may also add an extra 1cm, to make sure the *stress point guard* reaches the top without problems, this can be trimmed off later when removing the extra length of the zip.

If in doubt it is always good practice to make panels/pieces in paper and lay them on top of a panel to see how they fit together.

Join your *stress point guard* centre/out, using the *caterpillar technique*.

Make sure that you leave enough room for the *slider* to go up and down with ease and allow a 1cm joining onto the main panel. Fig 50 opposite.

It is the same technique for adding stainless steel or plastic zips to your outfit.

Fig 50

Fig 51 below shows a complete *stress point guard* and also a *zip guard*.

Fig 51

A *zip guard* is to prevent any flesh or hairs from getting caught in the zip and protect from any indentation or other discomfort. It should be 6cm wide and 1cm longer then the *stress point guard*.

The *zip guard* should only be joined to the bottom and right side of the zip, starting 5mm below the *stress point guard*.

Now is the perfect time to trim the excess length off the zip. The benefit of having left the zip a little longer means you can now trim each side individually, resulting in the perfect finish. Be careful when adding the stoppers.

Fig 52

If you have a long zip, as in a catsuit, it does reduce elasticity, especially if it goes through your body rise, from one side of the body to the other. So ensure you have compensated for this reduction of electricity by adding an allowance to your pattern: of 2cm horizontal ease at the hips.

In Fig 52 above, you will note that the *stopper* is on the outside of the panel, in the zip groove, so that it does not press into your back. Also, the zip has been nicely shaped at the bottom; as it will be visible as an indentation.

Press studs and eyelets

Press studs and eyelets are a good alternative to opening an outfit if you prefer not to have a zip. They are also effective as embellishments. Studs may be applied by various methods.

1. 'Press fasteners', are often the first choice when starting, due to their cheapness. They are a foldable bit of plastic that you place the studs in and then hit it with a hammer. Generally not recommended as it is difficult to get the right pressure which means you spoil the stud, and probably smash your thumb in the process. Fig 53 below.

Fig 53

2. A special pair of pliers with *dies (the steel area where you place your studs into)* at the end. These pliers often have a little wheel, like a windmill with several *dies*, allowing you to choose from several sizes. Place the studs in one of the *dies* at the end and squeeze firmly together, like a pair of pliers. Good but very limiting with the type/shape of stud/eyelet that can be used but useful if only a couple of sizes are required.

3. *Bench press stud tool.* Ideal to attach or clamp to a bench top and you can add any *die* required, allowing you to join any stud or eyelet. Fig 54 overleaf.

Eyelets allow you to pass material through latex, such as shoe laces. They need to be reinforced holes, so that the latex will not stretch and the eyelets simply pop out and are made following the same principles as studs.

I recommend the *bench stud press tool*, as you can fix any type of stud or eyelet: it's easy to use and not that expensive. It should be available via the Internet and at most haberdasheries.

Fig 54

Step 21 Preparation for studs

If a stud was added directly to the latex, when the latex was pulled it would stretch and the stud would just pop out. To prevent the latex from stretching, you have to add a little bit of *cotton tape*.

The *cotton tape* must stick to the latex and so it needs to be soaked in *PVA glue*, just as for zips. I would recommend applying the *PVA glue* to a long strip of *cotton tape* and then cutting off required lengths. See Fig 55A below and Fig 55B overleaf and see Fig 55C-D overleaf. This saves a lot of time.

Cotton tape normally comes in a roll, is 1cm wide and is very cheap.

Applying the *PVA glue*. *Fig 55A*

Soaking the *cotton tape* with *PVA glue.* *Fig 55B*

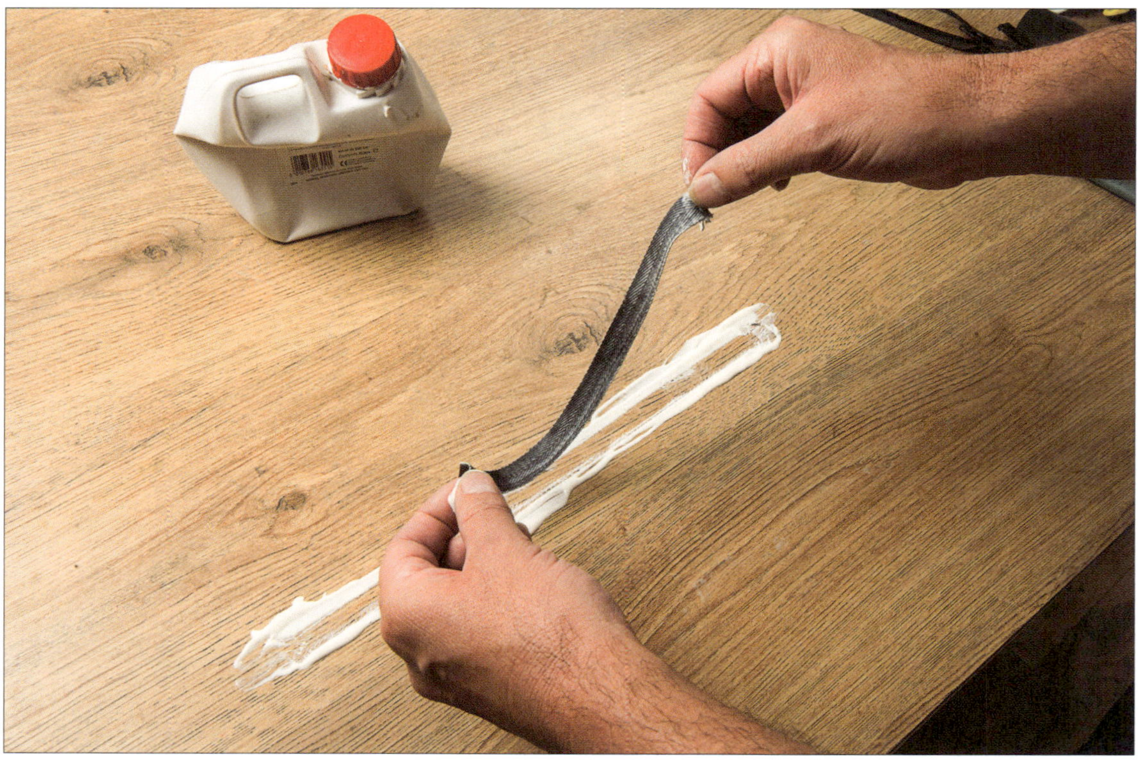

Putting the tape in a safe place to dry before soaking the other side. *Fig 55C*

A roll of cotton tape before gluing and how the *cotton tape* looks after the *PVA glue* has dried. *Fig 55D*

Prep the latex as normal. Cut the *cotton tape* to size, normally a length of 1.5cm per individual stud. However, you can use a whole length of *cotton tape.* This will severely restrict elasticity and even movement which could be ideal if used at the front of a shirt if you have a large stomach. It would prevent the studs from forming little peaks under the natural stress of the shape. The *cotton tape* goes on the inside; place it where the stud is going to be, using a pair of tweezers. Example Fig 56 overleaf.

Fig 56

Next carefully place a *stress point guard* on top. Work from the centre/out to push any *air bubbles* out. Fig 57 below. Then roller, talcum powder and wipe with *thinner*.

Fig 57

Step 22 Adding studs

Check the diameter of the stud cylinder. Make a same width hole through the latex and *cotton tape*, so that the stud can be positioned into it. This facilitates the squashing of the two halves of the stud easily and accurately together. Fig 58 below shows the making of the hole and Fig 59, overleaf, the cylinder of a stud poking through the latex and *cotton tape*.

Then place the top half of the stud on, see Fig 60 overleaf and place in the *bench press stud tool*. Fig 61 overleaf.

Just like a hole punch. *Fig 58*

Fig 59

Fig 60

Fig 61

Now press together. See Fig 62 below.

Fig 62

Once you have pressed them together, if it is not obvious whether they are tight enough, see if you can get a fingernail in between the stud and latex. You should not be able to do so, as the stud must be firmly next to the latex.

It is always a good idea to double check and test whatever you are doing as you go along. Hold alternate sides of the latex where the stud is and pull. The stud will separate at some point and one side is likely to hit you. It's more of a surprise than painful, but you could wear gloves as protection. But you will see that the stud will stay perfectly in place. Fig 63 below.

It is the same process for adding eyelets.

Fig 63

Buckles and other sorts of fasteners

Buckles come in a multitude of varieties and are all easy to fit.

On one side of the latex there are the eyelets and on the other side is the basic buckle.

All eyelets need to be reinforced with *cotton tape*, using the same process as for studs.

For the buckle side, all that is needed is to thread the latex strap through the buckle, fold the latex back upon itself on the inside, giving a 2-3cm *stress point guard*. No need for *cotton tape*.

Make sure that the latex goes the complete width, plus 1mm at each side of the buckle, otherwise the buckle will have a tendency to slide into one corner of the strap under any stress. Fig 64A below is before you have folded the strap upon itself. Note the professional finish. The end of the strap is curved into a nice arc so it will not get caught and come undone. Any indentation will also look so much nicer. Fig 64B overleaf shows the outcome if you did not add 1mm to the width of each side of the strap.

Fig 64A

Perfect width but see what will happen if you do not add 1mm to each side. *Fig 64B*

Fig 64C below shows you how it should look after adding 1mm to the width of each side of the strap, by the buckle.

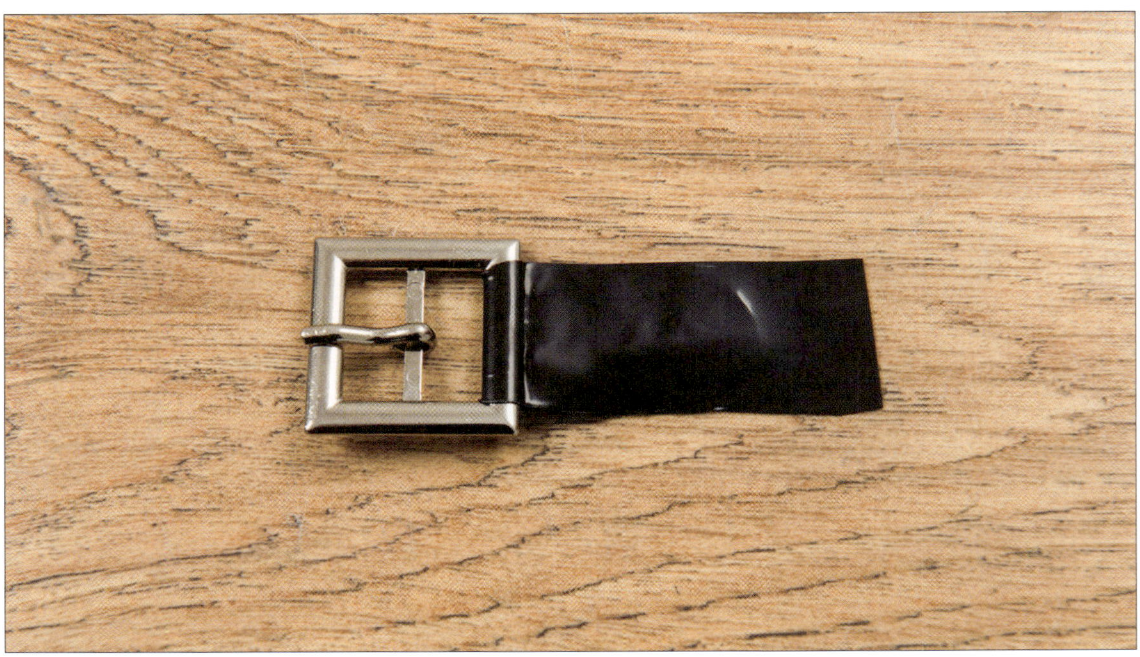

Fig 64C

Corsets

Corsets require boning to keep their shape. The boning is normally stainless steal, although some plastics are now also available. Stiff stainless steel boning comes pre-coated, either fixed lengths or on a roll which you then have to cut and file the ends until smooth. Now place in position and add *stress point guards*. There is also flexible boning, comes in a roll and requires cutting into lengths. To prevent sharp edges it is capped, either with a plastic or metal cap, and inserted into *cotton tape* sleeves. Fig 65 below is an example of this type of boning.

Add *PVA glue* to these cotton sleeves. Then they are ready to be sandwiched in between two pieces of latex, forming a *stress point guard*, to maintain the shape of your corset; normally this boning goes along the seam lines.

Busks, the opening to a corset with latches, are a little different, you just have to make tiny holes, in the latex, for the latches to go through and then fold the busk around on itself within the latex two times, should be enough. Then add a *stress point guard*. I would make a corset with eyelets first, then to make a corset with busks.

Fig 65

Diamontés and Braiding

Step 23 Adding a diamonté

Diamontés are normally so small they will not stress your outfit and so you can stick them anywhere. But the glue you use must be very strong, a *superglue*.

When applying diamontés or anything with *superglue*, be extra careful as it will set very quickly indeed and can leave a terrible mess. The way to pick up diamontés is with a pen or pencil with some Blu-Tack on the end. Fig 66A below.

Fig 66A

Only apply a tiny bit of *superglue* to each diamonté. Fig 66B opposite. Stick it directly onto the cleaned but not glued latex. Make precise marks where you want your diamontés to go, for accuracy. The diamontés will cover any marks. Fig 66C opposite.

Diamontés are long-lasting and a lot can be added to a small area without causing any overall stress.

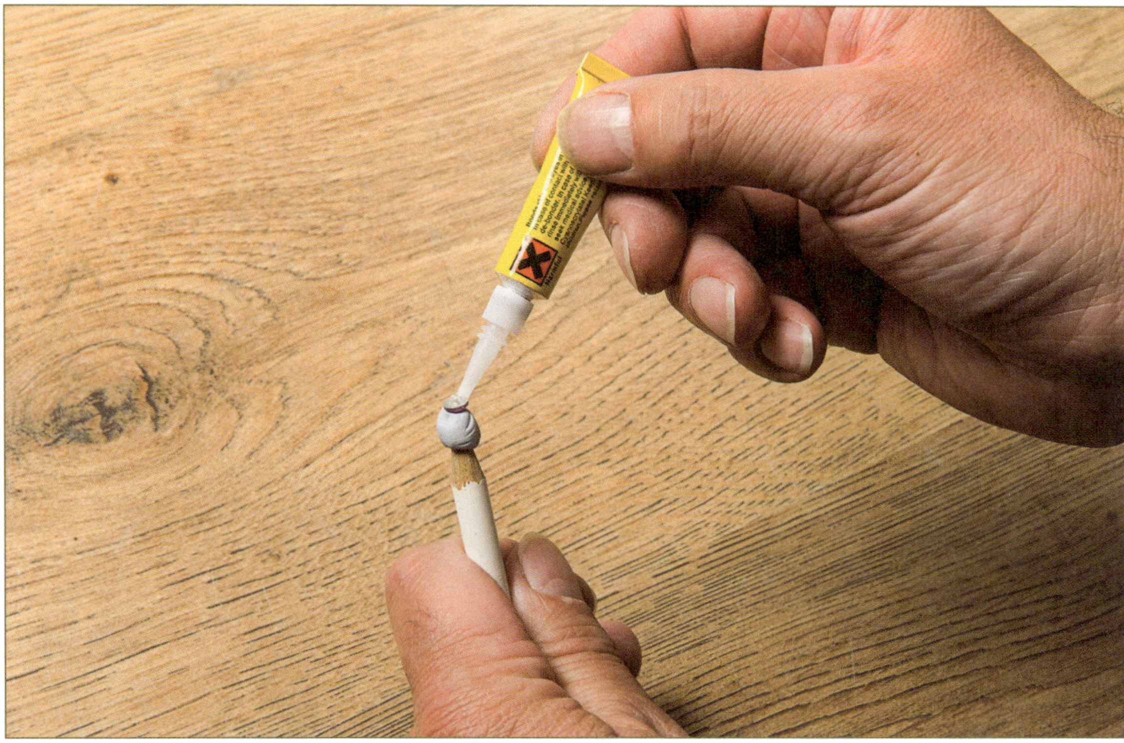

Fig 66B

Fig 66C

Step 24 Adding braiding

As with diamontés, latex glue isn't suitable for sticking braiding. *PVA glue* may well discolour your braiding, so again *superglue* is the best answer. The areas where braiding is placed generally have little stress or tension, for example, the ends of sleeves or tops of collars. However, please note that it restricts elasticity and can be very brittle.

Fig 67

Measure and lay out the braiding next to its position. Practise where it is going to go without any glue. Once the latex is cleaned, you can mark where the braiding will go, so long as you are sure that your marks will not be seen, that is, hidden by the braiding. Quickly line the latex with *superglue*. Fig 67 above. Be careful as if you make a mistake then it's a big problem. Also, be careful not to stick yourself to your outfit! It is *superglue*!

Next stick the braiding to the latex as quickly as possible. Fig 68 on the page opposite. You can use the *caterpillar technique* to safely and quickly apply braiding.

Rarely it is better to apply the glue to the braiding rather than the latex, for example, with long ruffles. Generally done only as an after thought to enhance your outfit. In such cases be careful not to let the glued braiding touch the latex where it shouldn't, otherwise it will leave a glue spot.

Fig 68

Fig 69

Braiding is generally an easy, quick, enjoyable process that can make a huge difference to an outfit. Fig 69 on the previous page is an example.

For ultimate control apply braiding by hand. But when handling diamontés always use the Blu-Tack approach.

Buttons, beads and brooches

These, including the buttons, are for decorative purposes only. They cannot be sewn directly onto latex, not even with adding *cotton tape* as a *stress point guard*, as if you sew through the latex it will still cause excessive local stress and tension, like a pin in a balloon, resulting in tearing. The solution is to sew the decorations onto a separate piece of latex first.

Step 25 Adding sewn buttons

The aim is to reduce the stress and tension to a manageable level. Sew the buttons onto a small piece of 0.4mm latex and then trim the latex so that it cannot be seen. Then glue it, as usual, to the panel of your outfit. The process of attaching latex to latex spreads the stress/tension giving enough elasticity that if the buttons are caught or pulled then they will not rip any latex. The stress/tension has diffused with the pyramid effect.

Latex to latex always provides the best stress relief as you are putting like with like. *Cotton tape* would not provide the stress disbursement required, it would just provide strength which is not useful in this situation. This technique will not harm the main outfit or make it uncomfortable, quite the opposite. Fig 70 opposite.

This approach is suitable for buttons, beads and broaches, and makes it look as though the items are really sewn on, giving a quality look to the outfit. Sewing directly into or through latex is never recommended, not even for reinforcing zips.

Fig 70

How to join other fabrics to latex

Step 26 Adding non-latex material

If the fabric is going to be used like an appliqué then it should be coated on the underside with *PVA glue*. *Prep* the latex area on your outfit with *latex glue*. On your outfit be careful not to have too much at the edge of the appliqué area, as any excess will have to be cleaned off, not always an easy task. A good tip is to mark where the appliqué is to go with your gel pen. Mark your latex 0.5cm before the edges of the appliqué seams so the appliqué will cover the pen marks. Only apply *latex glue* to up to these marks. The appliqué can now be applied and you will not have to clean off any area for excess glue.

If the non-latex material is going to be used at an end line, like an inside frill at the bottom of a skirt, then the fabric should be coated, where it will be joined, on both sides and have a *stress point guard* applied in the usual manner.

Texture

Providing texture to the latex can enhance an outfit. Different types of trim can be used for this, even something like curtain cord. Use on hat brims, neck lines, sleeves and down coat collars. Fig 71 below is part of the revel of an old morning suit, I made.

Fig 71

If you want the effect to be on the whole panel you can buy textured latex sheet, which looks a little like a tyre tread, if you want to make something very different. You can also make your own latex panels with liquid latex.

HEMS AND END LINES

Once an outfit has been made, the end line may not be in a perfect straight or smooth line. This is not uncommon. There are several ways to make end lines straight, apart from cutting them.

Trim

Trim can be used to make an end line seem straight, cleverly doubling up as a *stress point guard*. Trim can be added anywhere. You can make it yourself even using a *wave blade* for extra style but an easier solution is to buy it. Trim is available in various colours and widths, all 0.4mm thick, which is fine. Fig 72 below.

Trim can really add style. See the *rolled pleats* in Fig 40 on page 58. As with appliqués trim may reduce the elasticity of an area.

Fig 73A overleaf shows adding trim to the end line to hide any imperfections.

Fig 73B overleaf shows how trim adds style.

Fig 72

Fig 73A

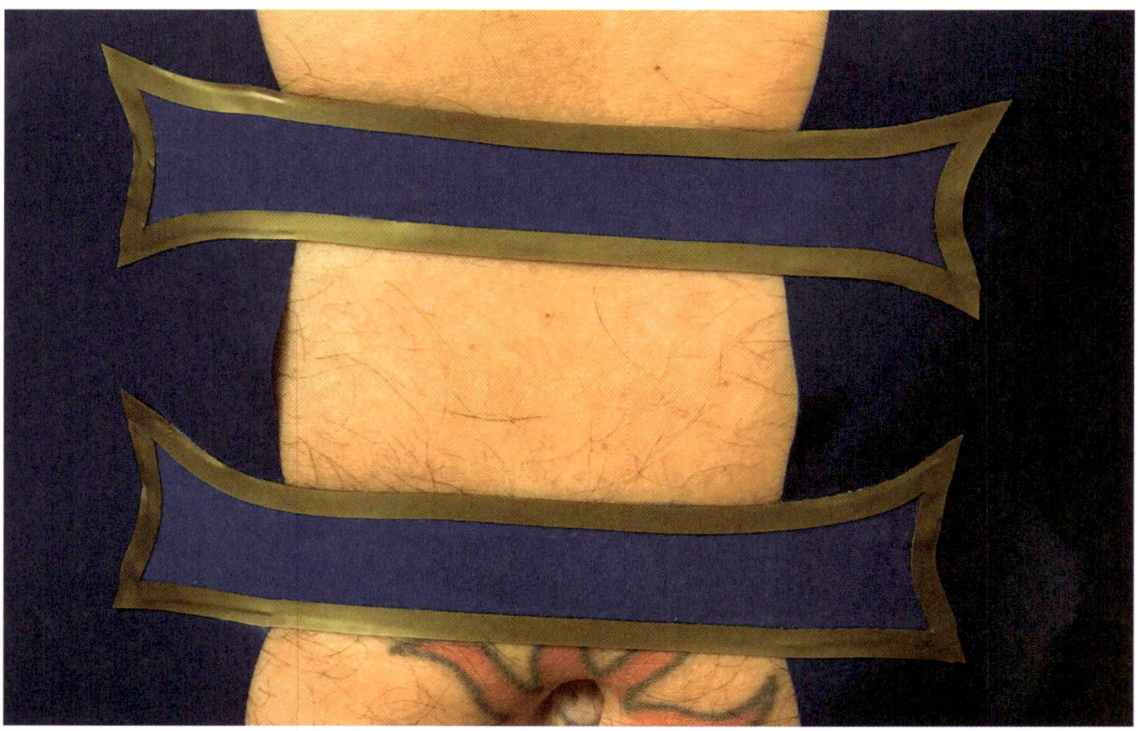

Fig 73B

Fold over

If adding trim does not give the required look to an end line and adding other fabric is not suitable, then there is the fold over technique.

Folding over the edge may be considered to be like a hem. Folded inwards gives a thinner sharper edge, not as nice as the standard natural look of an end of latex. If folded outwards you must make sure that the fold over trim is of a consistent width.

Simply *prep* the outside a little more than twice the required fold over trim width. Then making sure the glue is very dry, fold over, holding the latex between the thumb on top and index finger in the fold, at an angle of about 45 degrees. Join at a brave speed. This will help prevent getting any *air bubbles*.

I would recommend trying everything but would generally not recommend this fold over technique which is like a hem, as this really is not easy to do. Importantly, it does not look special even when you get a good result. Fig 74 below.

Finally, remember that a pleat or ruffle made of any fabric may, always be added to the end line.

Fig 74

Repairs

The skills and techniques I have shared with you will enable you to repair any damage sustained to your latex outfit.

Appliqués are very useful for covering up holes or small tears: they can be creatively shaped, for example into a lightning bolt, or the hole itself can be shaped into a keyhole and the appliqué placed on the inside or you can create a keyhole. This trick will transform any defect into an attractive feature/ embellishment. Fig 33, on page 47, shows appliqués. Fig 35, on page 49, shows keyholes.

If the tear or hole happens to be substantial, and is too large that it can not be disguised or covered with an appliqué or keyhole, then you shall have replace the whole panel. Undo the seams and there is your template. To undo seam lines, remove the *stress point guards* and carefully push a *thinner*-soaked *lint-free cloth* along the seam, gently separating the seam a centimetre or two at a time. For the most control only hold the seam close to the point that is being separated and do not pull apart from a 10cm distance.

It is important not to rush this, as it is a delicate procedure, although it should not give any lasting problems.

Alterations

If an outfit doesn't fit anymore or if you would like to tweak its style, it's easy to undo the seams. If for instance you need to make an outfit that is too big a bit smaller, while wearing the outfit, mark the areas to be trimmed off with a gel pen. Next, undo the seams, trim off the excess and glue the seams together again.

If you need to enlarge or widen an outfit that is too tight, then you can add an extra panel or replace a panel with a bigger panel. Both could be of a different colour or even gauge, then it will seem like a new outfit.

BEST WORKING PRACTICES – A RECAP

A recap

Before you start anything you should always think safety first. Make sure that your work surface is safe, your room is sufficiently ventilated and that you have enough space to carry out each task.

1. Use a good uncluttered work surface and allow enough time: better not to leave making your outfit until the day before you have to wear it.

2. Be clear about what you want to do and have everything you will need to hand.

3. Actions should be performed away from yourself, especially when using the rotary cutter. But when cutting away from yourself make sure you don't go towards your fingers. Keep all of you safe.

4. Hold the latex next to where you are going to cut, to get the most control.

5. Cut all lines freehand – don't use rulers or anything to help guide your rotary cutter.

6. When cutting latex, start 1cm away from the latex so the rotary cutter blade is already turning.

7. If cutting an arc shape, turn the latex and not your body. Try not to move your elbow outwards too much, concentrate on cutting a straight line away from yourself.

8. Seam actions start with an *anchor point*, whether cleaning, gluing or joining.

9. Clean a 1.5cm seam with one firm wipe.

10. Glue a 1 cm seam line. Dip your spatula into the glue, like a hen peck to get 3/4mm of glue onto the tip. Then press the spatula, holding it like a pen/pencil – with just two fingers – gently hold down, until nearly flat on the latex seam. Making a seam quickly will get the best results.

11. To check if glue has dried, use the finger tap test. If the seam has curled over or has just stuck to itself, you MUST wait until it is dry and then unfurl. Using a pair of tweezers will get better results than fingers. Also, use Blu-Tack with super glue when required.

12. The underneath latex seam MUST be as straight a line as possible. As well as the golden rule for seam lines, this is also extremely helpful when cutting around corners or a sharp bend, for example, like a 'V-neck' panel.

13. When joining seams using the *caterpillar technique* occasionally check that your seam is 1cm by **feeling** rather than **looking**. This way you will avoid stretching the latex.

14. If joining a long seam use a piece of paper to ensure that the seams do not stick together. A4 is generally a good size. If making something very large rather than using several pieces, acquire one large sheet. Wallpaper liner, 1m in width, is ideal and it is also good for making patterns.

15. Make sure that you are in control of your latex at all times. Normally this requires you to only be holding a small area. When making your *anchor point*, make sure that the edges you are holding are the smallest, that is, do not try to join a seam with a triangle which sticks out, as it will wiggle, try turning the seam over.

16. Never stretch latex, something easy to do without noticing especially when joining curves. Use *notch marks* with a white gel pen to make sure you are joining seams equidistantly. If your outfit, for example leggings, twists then the reason is nearly always that you have stretched one panel on the seam lines when gluing.

17. Once you have joined seams together by the *caterpillar* or *rolling techniques*, then use a roller to squash the seams together. This will remove any air bubbles and ensure a good join.

18. Add talcum powder and wipe it along the seams to stick to any excess glue. Remove the talcum powder with a *lint-free cloth*, dabbed with *thinner*, in one firm stroke. If there is still any excess, wipe the glue from your top panel to your bottom panel. This will prevent the *thinner* getting into your seam line and spoiling it.

19. Apply *stress point guards* at the end of every seam, under the crutch and *armscye* and on any other areas that might need it, like the V-neck of a shirt.

20. Be very careful when using *superglue*. As mentioned in 11 use Blu-Tack on the end of a pen/pencil or when applying super glue directly to the cleaned latex, do so in measured lengths – so that it does not harden.

21. Use *cotton tape* to prevent the latex from stretching when applying studs or eyelets.

22. To clean latex use *Perv-O-Shine* with a *lint-free cloth*. Do not use *thinner*.

23. Only gloss once at your destination, it is better to use a silicone lubricant to be applied with clean hands.

When adding non-latex fabrics onto latex

A. If the fabric is going to be placed onto your outfit as an appliqué, take note of any stress and tension. Generally just apply *latex glue* to your latex outfit and *PVA glue* the fabric side to be stuck. You must always glue both pieces.

B. If the fabric is going to be incorporated into the outfit, like a frill at the end line, it will have a *stress point guard* and so you need to apply the *PVA glue* to both sides of the fabric. *Prep* your panel as usual. Then add the fabric to your panel and then add your *stress point guard*, all as usual.

C. Certain fabrics will not absorb *PVA glue* and so superglue must be used. It is rather brittle and so should only be used for small surface areas and low tension/stress points such as when adding braiding to a collar or sleeve, or small items like diamontés. These are to be applied with Blu-Tack on the end of a pen/pencil, not with a pair of tweezers and never fingers.

D. Extra skills, such as sewing. Buttons can be sewn onto a small piece of latex which can then be glued onto an outfit. This disburses the stress. The same process can be used to create outfits without studs or zips but joined with Velcro or even magnets. Just place the magnets into a cotton tube, as used for corsets, sew either side so they do not move from their position, *PVA glue* the cotton tube, add the *stress point guard*. When taking any action with your panels it is always good practice to start top/down or front/back or centre/out.

Manufacturing norms

Zips: non-stainless steel for men are known as plastic zips, they have large teeth, and for women are known as nylon zips, with smaller teeth. Men's stainless steel zips have larger teeth than those for women. Zip openings are usually at the front for men and at the back for women.

Advice for seams when using thin latex

When gluing, the thinner the latex the greater tendency for it to curl up. When cutting 0.25mm always allow a 1.5cm seam, not the usual 1cm. Then cut off the 0.5cm excess once the glue has dried. This gives a perfect, neat, problem-free edge, very efficiently.

TO MAKE PERFECT PATTERNS FOR LATEX

Taking measurements

Always measure against your skin, for example from your neck line to waist, in a state of undress, either naked or in swimwear. Do not pull the tape measure taut, press it against your spine. This will be your true length. A good idea is to always tie a piece of string around your natural waist line, which is just below your ribs, making sure it is parallel to the floor. This will help you see all other measurements are accurate, ie, horizontal or perpendicular to the waist line.

A list of measurements and where to get them from will be shown in all pattern books and online.

Patterns

Most people start with the very good idea of copying clothing. I recommend progressing to make your own block pattern. There are some very good books available which show you how to do this. It is not difficult. If you can follow a recipe when making a cake then you can make bespoke clothing.

Helpful understandings

1. The patterns we have today have been developed over hundreds years – from improvements tailors have made, through basically trial and error. We are now at a standard that makes it very easy for everyone.

2. For a perfectly fitting bespoke pattern, follow the instructions. There is always an illustration to cross reference those instructions. All you have to remember is that all vertical measurements stay the same. But every horizontal measurement has ten per cent negative *ease; this is for latex up to 0.6mm, per common practise*. This simply means that you minus ten per cent from all horizontal measurements. When the parameter (width of the block) is being set, the bust line, I always add 2cm of *ease*, instead of what the book tells me, as I find it gives a much better fit, up to about size 16. All other, usually tiny, *ease* should be applied as directed. With bought patterns, just remember to minus ten per cent off all horizontal measurements. But I find it much easier to make my own patterns.

We do not take any ease off of any vertical measurements as this would make us hunch up. But we do take ease off of horizontal measurements to make sure that your outfit fits like a second skin; close fitting outfits are known as jersey fitting outfits.

Latex clothes have unique attributes, based on their elasticity. It is easier to make a new outfit than try to change a prototype outfit (*toile*). If you want to practise, a sensible tip is to do so using cheaper latex, this usually means 0.4mm, black latex.

Making a latex outfit is very enjoyable, even when you are gaining experience. Latex is very forgiving and you will see it come together quickly.

Making patterns

There are three ways of making a pattern and most enthusiasts start off in the order listed below. Whichever one you prefer it is good practice to always make sure you write everything down as you go along.

1. Reverse engineering

A brilliant idea: use existing clothes as a pattern. But take the measurements of the seams when you are wearing them. Vertical measurements are the same but you need to minus ten percent from your horizontal measurements.

2. Flat pattern making

Soon you will start to have ideas beyond your clothes. So you can just use your actual body measurements. Nipples are called *points* and so the *centre point* is exactly between the two. Start from your *central point, draw a vertical line* and measure yourself at strategic places, bust line, natural waist, upper hips, hips or seat as it known for men but it is the same thing (the widest part of your bottom) and copy those measurements, with the ten percent horizontal negative ease adjustment, onto some paper. Then make your outfit.

3. Block patterns

This is the method I recommend. You will end up with a master pattern of your body. Allowing you to trace over it and then from this duplicate create your outfit. Keep your master pattern safe, to use over and over again, allowing you to create new and different outfits quickly and easily.

Measurement golden rules

Vertical measurements, stay the same.

Horizontal measurements.

The three VERY IMPORTANT steps to always check.

Your horizontal measurements will usually be (1) divided by two, unless stated by the book, as the block is only half of your body, then minus the (2) ten percent horizontal negative ease and then see if there is (3) any *ease*, given by the book, to be added or taken away.

Ease has simply originated from when during the passing of time, improvements were made to the pattern. These adjustments made improvements to one part but that meant it affected another different part of the pattern, so these different parts had to be moved back again. When wearing a top with a collar, if you lift the front of your collar the sides of your front panel will go towards the middle. To keep the same shape but with a higher collar, you would have to move the waist back out. This adjustment would be written as 'minus ease for the waist line' in a standard pattern book.

Understanding latex patterns

Unlike other fabrics, latex does not have a grain. It is elastic and likes to go back to its original shape and size once stretched, pulling towards its central point. This elasticity can be used to great advantage, for example, to flatten a stomach or give a better cleavage.

As latex is known as a *jersey fit* material you should choose pattern options that say 'close fitting'.

A dart has been added to obtain a perfect fitted 3D pattern on a 2D surface.

Assembling your patterns

Every panel should be marked with white gel pen lines, known as *notch marks*, so that when joining your panels together there are guide lines to make sure everything is equidistant. No stretching. You make notch marks by making holes in you pattern with a hole punch about 2cm in from the edge on every horizontal line; bust, waist, hip and so on.

Assemble, Top/Down. Front/Back. Centre/Out.

Starting at the top, make sure that your *anchor point* is perfect. So any margin of error at the bottom can be easily managed. But double check the notch marks as you go along.

When making your outfit, the general practise is to place any front panel on top of the next panel. So front onto back.

When assembling your outfit, you should generally glue it into two independent halves. Then join the last two blocks, front and back, together. So start with your front shoulder seam onto back shoulder seam. Then your *armscye*, front half the back half. Then your side seams. NOTE, lastly, the sleeve seams.

Checking your outfit

You will reach a point when you have rolled your seams together, applied talcum powder and cleaned off any excess glue. Do not clean with *Perv-O-Shine*, just yet. Add *stress point guards* and now is the moment to try it on. It is likely to be a perfect fit, however . . .

If it is loose: If a seam is not tight enough anywhere, just mark the area with your gel pen, undo the appropriate seam and cut off the excess, *prep* and join it back together.

If it is loose from under the arm to your shoulder seam, giving an unwanted glimpse of your bust, shorten the seam line. Cut 0.5cm from either end. Cutting under the armscye may require you to cut 2/3cm down your side seam, as well as 0.5cm in, making a little triangle to be removed and rejoin. For your shoulder, unpeel the seam line, draw and cut the new line and stick it down again.

If a standard collar is a bit floppy, then apply the same principles as above at the collar's end line. The result will be to push up the middle fold, making it a much better collar.

If it is tight: Just change that panel or add a panel.

Gauges – what to wear?

Men – 0.4mm

Women – 0.5mm

The difference of thickness, arrives from its job. 0.5mm is much firmer and stretches less. Women usually have larger panels and so to have that extra bit of control is very useful. Also, women are much more curvaceous and so it is easier to control certain areas like the stomach and cleavage.

Catsuits are generally made from 0.5mm latex. This means that by the end of a long evening, your arms could ache at the inner elbow. So make your catsuit body in 0.5mm but the sleeves in 0.4mm. Mixing the gauges gives different ease of shape and movement to those areas.

Corsets: From 0.6mm to 0.8mm. However, 1.1mm can be used, it is down to the pattern and personal tolerance. Commonly corsets have laces and so you will be able to get to the right comfort.

Getting in/out of your outfit, plus, looking your best

It is a good idea to have a bath or shower before wearing latex. This will remove any perfumes, etc, and having clean skin will facilitate the gliding on of the latex. I also would recommend using a little silicone based lubricant over those areas of skin that come into the most contact. Some people use baby oil but this will eventually cause damage to your outfit.

I do not use talcum powder, as it tends to form clouds of dust putting it on and when you remove your outfit it can look a bit like plaster of Paris.

Another way to get in and out of your outfit is under a running shower, although this is usually for neck entry catsuits.

It is best not to polish your outfit until you are at your destination. Then, only shine with silicone lubricant; liquid is better than spray, using either a *lint-free cloth* or best of all, clean warm hands.

FASHION

Historically latex clothing has been connected with BDSM, fetishes and sexual play. The fashion and musical industry and some actors have adapted this very versatile material into their attire. Today, latex has assumed a socially accepted role, all-be-it a more deviant, on the edge one. Including film stars, top models and musicians. A quick look on the Internet will reveal a wealth of fetish style/fashion friendly clubs, where you can meet like minded people. The core ethic should be respect, simply that. If going to a club do not expect anything more than a smile, nor give reason to evoke anything more than a smile. Most clubs have a door policy where wearing latex is more often than not compulsory for admittance. It is definitely worth being adventurous and seeing this style of life.

Where to wear latex clothes

Most latex clothes are associated with fetish clubs, which are great fun. In true fetish clubs most people are friendly by nature and usually have genuine respect.

Naturally, latex is also great fun to wear at private parties and, at an appropriate level, in the more enlightened mainstream clubs.

There are a lot of social sites that will help, at any level, easily found on the Internet.

Maintenance and aftercare

1. Preparation prior to wearing

Avoid spraying any perfumes, cologne, body lotions or even hair sprays. Try to have your latex cleaned beforehand. Not shined. Clean with a good wipe with *Perv-O-Shine*, which is much cheaper if bought, as it is, *PVC dressing aid*.

Latex will look skin tight when you put it on and so not to worry if the outfit seems a little creased – wrinkles will go.

Jewellery and decorations – do not wear jewellery while getting in or out of an outfit as it might cause damage. If you perspire whilst wearing jewellery it might stain your outfit.

Coins – be aware, some stain.

Sharp objects – keep away from these as they could easily make a gash, ruining an outfit.

2. Stains

If your outfit is stained, then try cleaning with *Perv-O-Shine* and if there is still a stain/mark then try Magic Eraser, available from hardware shops. If still not removed try squashing a bit of latex of the same colour against it. The stain will leach into the new bit and so be lessened, and so on. The principle of bit biting – the stain/mark should halve. Problems are better avoided than fixed. Another solution is to add trim or an appliqué to cover/disguise the problem area. You could even make a keyhole if appropriate.

3. Once in your outfit

Once at your destination. Shine yourself using either silicone based spray or better still silicone based lubricant with either a *lint free cloth* or preferably clean warm hands.

STORAGE

Before storing, make sure that the outfit is in good condition. Clean with *Perv-O-Shine*, the best option, or even warm soapy water followed by towel drying – you must make sure everything is dry before storage. Soapy water may cause problems if your outfit has zips. Then wipe with silicone or lightly sprinkle with talcum powder.

Outfits can be hung on wooden hangers, ensure that nothing else adheres to or touches your outfit.

However, make sure that the the latex is not too heavy, like a catsuit, then there is a risk that the outfit may become misshapen and/or even stretched. You can carefully store your outfits in a draw. Making sure that they are in the dark. Keep away from temperature extremes, like the cold of a garden shed or heat of a radiator.

CONCLUSION

You now have all the information to inexpensively and yet professionally enjoy making your own bespoke latex clothing. Try to use block patterns as soon as possible, starting with the bodice, an easy leap to looking amazing.

Pattern cutting is part of the process of looking the best dressed person. Once you have a good pattern it can be adapted into many styles with only minor changes.

Latex is worn not by many but by a few who enjoy clothes that are on the cutting edge of style and fashion, sexy, chic – perfect for those who are pushing the boundaries of fashion, like models, musicians, fetishists or simply someone special.

Imagination is our liberation. Once you have that pattern which is not difficult, then the world is your oyster.

GLOSSARY

Air bubbles	Trapped pockets of air that can occur when joining and gluing.
Anchor point	The starting part of a seam line.
Armscye	The armhole, the circumference of your arm.
Bench press stud tool	A tool to press studs or eyelets onto your outfit.
Caterpillar technique	The usual method for joining latex seams.
Centre point	In between your points, your nipples.
Cleaner 4 or thinner	Bostik 6009 in Europe is the best for cleaning prior to gluing. For local solvents please look on appropriate social sites.
Cling film	Applied to keep food fresh. Known in Northern American as Saran or plastic wrap.
Cotton tape	100% cotton tape on a roll used for preventing elasticity, such as when adding studs.
Dies	The different *steel* presses that allow you to press studs and eyelets, etc, together.
Ease	A given measurement to promote a better fit.
Fin	A piece of latex which has been joined together and is going to be stuck to a seam, making a pleat.
Glue-balls	Tiny balls of glue usually generated when cleaning the work surface. They can easily stick to a seam and are best removed with tweezers.
Glue - Latex glue	Bostik 3851 in Europe, the strongest glue, it is 100% natural, therefore biodegradable. However, PVA glues, which are man made, like Copydex, are also fit for the purpose. For local glues please look on appropriate social sites.

Glue-strings	Seen when the glue has been joined and separated before drying or if a panel is moved from its work surface position after the applied glue has dried or on your spatula if using old glue.
Hill kinks	These occur when a seam has been joined and there is an excess of latex on one side, making the seam undulate.
Hole entry	The entrance point of an outfit.
Jersey fit	A tailoring term that means fabric that is close fitting to the body.
Jump	When joining latex together, instead of continuously joining a seam you lift your finger or thumb and leave a space, usually resulting in kinks.
Latex glue	See, *Glue - Latex glue*
Lint-free cloth	Usually a medical cleaning cloth that does not leave any fibres behind.
Mountain kinks	When a seam has been joined together and there is a severe excess of latex on one side, looking like a mini *fin*.
Notch marks	Little gel pen marks which give a measurement of distance on a seam. There should be a notch mark on both panels so when you arrive at a certain point you can see that the seam has been joined equidistantly. If it is over 2cm out then you have to go back to the previous *notch mark* and start again.
Rolled pleat	A new type of pleat when the *fin* is not completely stuck to itself.
Paper separation	To insert a piece of paper in between seam lines or appliqués to prevent them from sticking to each other prematurely.
Perv-O-Shine	This is a vanilla smelling, blue liquid which cleans off talcum powder, gel pen marks and even grass stains. It is much cheaper if bought as *PVC dressing aid*.

Points	Nipples. So your *Centre Point* is in between your nipples.
Prep	To prepare seams by cleaning and applying glue, done on both panels to be joined.
PVA glue	Copydex in Europe. For local solvents please look on appropriate social sites. A man-made glue, usually white and rather smelly. Used mostly for soaking into cotton tape, so that it will stick to latex. PVA glue can also be used for gluing seams together although not as strong as Bostik 3851.
PVC dressing aid *What is sold as Perv-O-Shine*	Something that cleans latex quickly, easily and thoroughly.
Rolling technique	Alternative to the *caterpillar technique*, used when joining a latex seam when the curve is too severe.
Sliders	Mechanism for opening and closing zips.
Stoppers	These are at the end of zips. They will be little metal clamps or melted plastic.
Stress point guard	An extra small bit of latex added to prevent the latex from coming apart at stress points, for example, to be added to the ends of seam lines.
Thinner or cleaner 4	Bostik 6009 is the best for cleaning prior to gluing. For local glues please look on appropriate social sites.
Tin foil	Aluminium, commonly used in baking.
Toile	A prototype outfit.
Wave blade	A normal rotary cutter blade, but rippled to give a wavy edge instead of a straight line.
Zip guard	A panel of latex that will protect you from catching flesh, hair or having a zip indentation.

AUTHOR BIOGRAPHY

Since the beginning of my thinking days, I have noticed that I have always been a little different, sometimes to my great delight and at other times to my deep dismay. But I wouldn't have it any other way.

My life has been a series of largely happy accidents. I travelled the world for eight years, having many an adventure, some planned but mostly sent upon me, as though I was in the *Iliad*! My charmed life has allowed me to survive from being stranded in the Himalayas in winter, to survive encounters with many wild and poisonous animals, to see the wonders of the world, made both by humans and nature. Also, to enjoy festivals, like the Day of the Dead, in Mexico. I have been to most countries and lived in South Africa, Hong Kong and the United Kingdom. It was my intension to learn the different ways of the world whilst seeing its wonders.

We are not here for a long time, just a good time. So every year I have a new experience, like travelling to Germany to go in a Zeppelin or starting to keep bees. As well as fully enjoying local life.

I have largely been self employed as originally I found it hard to get a job. I then realised I'm rather good at business. Being a natural day dreamer and never listening to anyone who says that it can't be done, I just succeeded.

My life has been a very full and lucky one. Now, I wish to share my luck by sharing my knowledge and experiences.